KILTOLOGY

Words of Wisdom for the Kilted Universe

Volume II

A Few Drams Later...

By Kevin M. Thompson

KiltsRock.com

Published by BOTK Publishing

Edited by

Cover Photography by Denzil Ernstzen Photography

ISBN: 0985938226

ISBN-13: 978-0-9859382-2-2

I am dedicating this book to all the First Responders out there. The Police, Firemen, EMTs and every other person who runs at trouble when everyone else is running away.

These good people put their lives on hold while they rescue ours.

They deserve our unending gratitude and thanks.

Be Safe.

CONTENTS

Read the contents section from Volume I.

I don't want to write it out again.

Each entry is a direct
Reflection of my mood
When I wrote it.

You will find I
Have been frustrated and cranky
More than once
While writing
This book.

Be Strong.

Put a Kilt On.

Let the shenanigans begin…

Kiltology #201

If you are ever able to get into one of those money machines where wind blows money around for you can catch, a kilt is probably not in your best interest.

Aside from the obvious issues of your kilt turning into a parachute and scaring the thin-skinned, you will most likely not catch very much as the kilt will be in the way.

You will, on the other hand, make more from tips as you exit the machine than what you caught in the thing!

❧

Kiltology #202

A wise man once asked, "Who is the more foolish, the fool or the fool who follows him?"

I say neither. The more foolish is the idiot who spends countless hours pondering such questions instead of kilting up, getting out, and enjoying the world and all the things in it.

Unless, of course, that time spent pondering is over a favorite beverage in the company of good friends and family!!

Kiltology #203

The real reason the TSA has implemented the body scanners
is NOT for enhanced security.

They want to get the answer to "the question" without having
to ask the Kiltie or do a kilt check.

(Now you know why all the screeners have that silly grin
when you walk though the scanner in a kilt.)

CROSO

Kiltology #204

It is a little known fact that the telescopic mirror was NOT
invented for mechanical or medical investigation.

It was invented by a bright lass specifically to check up the
kilt of a young gent in the local pub without his knowledge.

Kiltology #205

Underwear was NOT invented simply to wear under p@nt$.

It is in fact a cruel torture device imposed upon the kilt-wearing world to reduce their procreation and make them generally unhappy.

The second part actually worked.

ॐॐॐ

Kiltology #206

A Kiltie was walking around and a smart-ass passer-by shouted, "Nice Skirt!"

The Kiltie responded:

THWAP
KA-POW
POP
THUD

"... and now you can tell yer other wise-ass friends you got yer ass kicked by a man in a skirt!"

Kiltology #207

When your four year old son says, "Daddy, you belly getting bigger," you know it is time to get on the kilted diet fast.

It is EXTREMELY expensive to ignore his advice and grow larger than your kilt. You can't just grab one at the local clothing store if you need a different size.

 C3 80

Kiltology #208

It is painfully well known that Monday's suck.

To help alleviate the pain, it is hereby decreed that the first workday of the week is now called "Maltday".

Should take the edge off going back to work a little.

Kiltology #209

Hunting turkey in a kilt is a very scary and dangerous idea.

The first thing you have to worry about is the other hunters who mistake your tartan for a turkey (yes, it can happen).

Then you have issue of hiding, especially if you are wearing any tartan from a mill where the reds run a little light in tone.

Worst of all is the act of hunting them. Squatting in the woods for a long time in a kilt invites all sorts of critters to find a home in the kilt you are so cozy in.

You really don't want anything trying to make a home in your kilt that wasn't there when you put it on!

CRSO

Kiltology #211

While the kilt offers protection for a great many things, it has no defense against large quantities of triptophan commonly found in the mountain of turkey we enjoy today.

I suggest donning the kilt with the straps a little looser than normal and having a flask handy.

You will need it to stave off the effects of too much turkey!

(The contents go in the coffee you have after you eat so you don't miss the game!)

Kiltology #212

Everyone has a nemesis. A Kiltie's nemesis is well made food, cold pumpkin pie in my case.

The love of good food will inevitably lead to the need for bigger kilts, which can get really expensive.

(I had to do this. Two whole pumpkin pies have mysteriously vanished from my fridge in the past 48 hours. I think there might be a wild haggis living in the house somewhere.)

☙❦❧

Kiltology #213

Coffee and donuts. 'Nuff said.

(And no, this is not the result of too much fun. Quinn and Addy are really energetic lately.)

Kiltology #214

It is said that for a man with a hammer, every problem looks like a nail.

For a man with a kilt, every problem is an excuse to gather other Kilties at the local gathering spot to talk about it over several beverages and eventually attack it with a caber-like tool of some kind.

Suffice it to say, Kilties have few problems that last more than a day in their original state.

෩

Kiltology #215

The power of mistletoe has been drastically underestimated for centuries by all but the Kilties.

Getting a kiss under the mistletoe is one thing. Wearing a mistletoe sporran ... well, just be warned that you best be single and sober if you dare wear it in public!

(If you are attached ... wearing a mistletoe sporran as you stand in the doorway to surprise your significant other as they come home is HIGHLY suggested!)

Kiltology #216

One thing every Kiltie is eventually forced to do is this:
organize the @#$%@#$% garage.

Why?

If you can get more crap out of the house and into the
garage, you have more space for kilts...

... and scotch cabinets and bikes and weapons and all manner
of kilted stuff!

(Yes, I'm doing this now. I expect to free up enough room
for at least a dozen or more kilts if anyone needs a prototype
tested!)

 CʒƧꝊ

Kiltology #217

Caffeine is, at the same time, the Kilties best friend and worst
enemy.

It is GREAT at getting things going after a rather extended
squawk when the average Kiltie is particularly slow to rise.

It is HORRIBLE when consumed too late, preventing said
Kiltie from enjoying a restful evening's sleep.

(It is even worse when consumed DURING the
aforementioned squawk. A drunk, hyper Kiltie may be the
single most destructive force on the planet next to Quinn.
I'm certain both caber tossing and golf were invented during
such squawks.)

Kiltology #218

For the single Kilties out there, this is the best workout I've ever seen!

1. Strap on a kilt
2. Get invited to a "Toy Party" (lots of women talking about sex toys while drinking alcohol of some kind.)
3. Show up to Toy Party in said kilt.

You are assured to expend a great deal of energy either trying to avoid really drunk women or "not" avoiding the bonnie lass in a tartan skirt who said hello with a glass of single malt.

One way or another, you will get one hell of a workout!

(Word of warning: DO NOT consume a great deal of alcohol before or during the party unless you plan to be the main attraction, in which case, you are on your own.)

☙ ❧

Kiltology #219

Patience is something almost every Kiltie must have lots of to deal with life in a kilt.

It is also what you call those who refuse to stop messing with kilt wearers, irritating and agitating them as much as they can.

Kiltology #220

More on how to stay warm while kilted:

1. Heavyweight wool kilt.
2. Bonnie lass.
3. Fire (but only if the first two aren't present).
4. Try working on #2 some more, even if you have #3.
5. Single malt (but only if you have #1 and #2. Mixing with #3 is a REALLY bad idea).
6. Phone a friend (obviously if you have reached this far, you have burned yourself, drank all the single malt, and scared away all the lasses!)

If you have gotten this far and are still freezing, find a tauntaun, gut it, and crawl inside. It won't matter what you smell like at this point.

⚜

Kiltology #222
Don't mess with a man in a kilt.

This is why:

(Yes, Utilikilts and chainsaws go very well together ...
especially if the guy wearing the kilt is as tall as the house
behind him!)

Kiltology #223

How to win any war without firing a single shot:

1. Feed a couple Kilties haggis, boiled eggs, and single malt ...
in that order.
2. Let them enjoy the evening.
3. Wake them up early the next day and send them into the
enemy camp.

The war should be over about 15 minutes later without a
single bullet ever being shot.

It can be argued that biological warfare was used,
but it is 100% organic and completely recyclable.

CB EO

Kiltology #224

Single malt fixes a great many things.

Today, unfortunately, it isn't curing this evil that wracks my
body.

Getting whatever the kids bring home from school is a
wicked evil that even the greatest of kilts cannot protect you
from!

Kiltology #225

The Harbinger of Doom, Bringer of Desolation and Destroyer of Worlds has been revealed and is now among us.

The Harbinger's name is █████, and she is destroying everything in reach.

(image redacted)

(The kilt has no defense against her. Run while you can, before *she* learns to run after you!)

(I have the camera on the fastest shutter setting ... that is how fast she is moving her hands to destroy everything!)

ℭℬℰ

Kiltology #226

When shoveling snow, be ever mindful of the neighborhood busybody.

It is almost assured that she will find an angle at which she can see your mistletoe and berries so she can call the cops for indecent exposure.

(If said busybody happens to be a kilt-loving, twentysomething female physical fitness instructor who seems interested and needs her driveways shoveled, I suggest the bend-and-scoop method. I'm certain she will come over and ask for some help.)

Kiltology #227

It is well known that a male's dancing prowess is one of many skills a female will consider when selecting a companion in many species, including our own.

We Kilties have a huge advantage here.

Instead of wild, convoluted movements to engage a female, a Kiltie need simply move his hips back and forth in a rhythmic fashion.

This movement will set the Kiltie's sporran swaying in a profoundly suggestive and hypnotic manner which is unlikely to be ignored by anyone, if it is done correctly.

Be warned. Doing so has no assurance that any attracted females are in fact the ones you were trying to attract.

ॐ ৪০

Kiltology #228
I have created a wonderful winter treat!!

What you need:
1. Bottle Laphroaig 10 year old
2. Egg Nog
3. Glencairn (or any other glass, but this one is best in my opinion).

How to make LaphroaigNog:
1. Add dram of Laphroaig to Glencairn (or other glass) as if you were going to drink it neat.
2. Top off glass with Nog.
3. Stir
4. Enjoy VERY carefully!

Kiltology #229

The power of the Kilt Compels You.

The power of the Kilt gives the wearer the ability to effectively officiate Sweater Puppy Races at the drop of a ... err ... hat?

The time, location, and entrants may be completely random, but the Official of the race does have final say in declaring a winner!

(And yes, these races can happen at the strangest places, such as the coffee shop, grocery store, or even the library!)

CℨℰႧ

Kiltology #230

The Power of the Kilt has many uses.

When shopping for that hard to find gift, here is a suggestion:

1. Bring a friend or two when shopping.
2. Locate item.
3. Show up in kilt to distract other shoppers.
4. Send friends in to get gifts while other shoppers are trying not to look at you in a kilt.

This can also be used in any situation where distraction is helpful. Proven to work when standing in line at the bar.

Kiltology #232

A lass asking "What do you want for Christmas?" is a question which has perplexed men for ages. Aside from what is known (more kilts, tools, cars, etc...) you never know what will get the best response from your lady.

Here is a simple, proven answer that will always get a giggle, blush, and usually a lot more!

"I don't want anything, but a smile on your face. If you insist on buying something, make sure I can get it off you with my teeth."

CB ED

Kiltology #233

While reveling this Christmas, be ever vigilant of how close you are standing to the fire.

The freedom of the kilt comes at a price as standing too close to the fire could unexpectedly roast your chestnuts.

I don't care how much you love the holidays, roasted chestnuts are no fun.

Merry Christmas

from the Brotherhood of the Kilt

Kiltology #234

Beware blushing lasses bearing Rudolf the Red Nose
Reindeer dolls with light-up noses.

They are only trying to find their way to the mistletoe hanging
'neath your kilt!

ೞ೩

Kiltology #235

Luckily for we kilted folks, sanity and reason are things that
are seldom expected of us.

Who goes to ask the people throwing trees and eating sheep
innards for intelligent advise?

(Funny part is, if you look at major inventions and
discoveries throughout history, it would have done the world
a lot more good to pay attention to the Kilties!)

(Funnier still, it seems this is completely wrong.
Sanity and reason are expected of me
all the time!)

Merry Christmas

from the

Brotherhood of
the Kilt

kiltsrock.com

Kiltology #236

The garage is every Kiltie's nemesis.

It is at the same time a black hole where things important to you go to vanish and where mountains of useless crap seem to be invading your home.

Make sure none of your kilts wind up in the garage. The resident tribe of scavengers will collect them and turn them into a shanty roof.

ೞ ೞ

Kiltology #237

All Kilties are genetically engineered to be superior to all others in their ability to nap well.

More so, according to some, than their ability to attract attention, consume vast quantities of strange food, and aggravate the p@nt-wearing male companions of women everywhere!

(And a word of warning ... never wake a napping Kiltie unless it is an emergency, such as free food, an offer of a pub crawl, or most importantly, if you happen to be a bonnie lass with a blue ribbon to award!)

Kiltology #238

Best Kiltie New Year's resolution ever:

"I resolve to rid myself of the bifurcated prison of the p@nt$ and help those who have yet to be freed see the light."

C8 80

Kiltology #239

There is a reason why you almost never see any news about violence among kilted folks.

Most people don't have the cojones to confront a man in a kilt, and those who do are unwilling to do so because they don't want to say they lost a fight they started with a man in a skirt.

(It also explains why kilts and bagpipes are considered weapons of war ... they can be very demoralizing to the enemy!)

Here is a great humorous example I've heard and found around the web.

(Giving respect to the original author, I chosent not to reprint the story as the author passed some time ago, making it impossible to gain direct permission. If you want to read the story all you need to do is go online and look up "The Lone Highlander". The story was printed in "Folktales Told Around the World" by Richard Mercer Dorson. The story itself starts on page 41. ISBN # 9780226158747 for those keeping track. ☺)

Kiltology #240

Be careful when choosing your kilt and accessories. Finding
the perfect kilt, only to wear a belt that is a bit too small, can
make you uncomfortable.

A kilted muffintop, no matter how awesome the kilt, is one
of the scariest sights to behold in all the world.

ॐ ॐ

Kiltology #241

It is a well proven fact that opinions are like buttholes ...
everyone has one (and some people have two at times.)

Furrycelt inspired me with this quote:

" Once I learned deep down that the opinions of total
strangers are meaningless, I felt a huge wave of freedom wash
over me."

Only when we stop trying to impress the masses and live our
own lives will we be truly be free. Kilt up and be free!

Kiltology #242

Housecleaning in a traditional wool kilt is not recommended unless you plan to wash your kilt when the house is clean.

Wool kilts are dirt magnets, and all the bending, kneeling, and moving around associated with housecleaning will surely soil the kilt.

That is, of course, unless you have a bonnie lass as an audience while you "clean". In that case, make sure you get that spot under the couch REALLY clean, she will appreciate it.

ᎤᏂᏐᏯ

Kiltology #243

It is a little known fact that a man in a kilt was the first to solve Chinese algebra whilst blindfolded.

The next day he woke up, took the blindfold off, pushed away the empty bottle, and looked at his work, bewildered.

Chinese algebra has not since been solved by anyone, with or without a blindfold.

Kiltology #244

No matter how many differences we Kilties may have
between us, it is a very well known fact that when the p@nt$
hit the fan, we come together as an unstoppable,
unified force!

No one can stop the Kilties!

ॐ৪০

Kiltology #245

Insanity can be described as trying to convince a Kiltie that
wearing a kilt is wrong.

That is about as effective as trying to attack an army of angry
wookies with a can of diet spam.

Kiltology #246

You only need three people to have a great time!

One person to drive
One person to bring the single malt
One person to be the idiot.

*It is common for the role of the idiot to spread to everyone as the evening goes on, especially if you bump into another group of people out for a great time.

CECED

Kiltology #247

Shag rug is evil, especially if you have children. It's only saving grace is its cool name.

(Advice to single Kilties: If a bonnie lass walks up and says, "Wanna shag?" or something close, stick around and talk to her unless she is completely repulsive. She likes your kilt a LOT.)

Kiltology #248

While under almost every other circumstance, Mother Nature
is our mother, who nurtures us and provides for us.

When a Kiltie is trudging around the glen, Mother Nature
becomes a blushing bonnie lass, doing whatever she can to
get a glimpse under the kilt!

Why do you think wind comes out of nowhere to blow your
kilt here and there on an otherwise calm, clear day?

☙❧

Kiltology #249

Contrary to popular belief, it is extremely difficult to do a
visual kilt check without either lifting the kilt in some manner
or sticking your head up it.

Just about everyone who cries indecent exposure has to put
in a serious amount of effort to actually see what ever it is
they think they saw.

(If you ARE going to stick your head up a kilt ... watch out
for Nessy or some other mythical beastie. BE WARNED!)

Kiltology #250

What a Kiltie wears under his kilt is this:

NONE OF YOUR #@$^@%^ BUSINESS!!!

Where is all the ruckus to get women to wear panties under their skirts all the time? If I am supposed to wear something under my kilt, why don't they?

Where is the ACLU when I need help with a good discrimination suit?

(If you *do* want to make it your business, make sure you warm your hands and ask nice.)

CŞŞƆ

Kiltology #251 - Kilted Sarcasm

Kilted Sarcasm is one of the most difficult languages to master. It is a combination of pseudo-eloquence, obscure vulgarities, and outright insanity all mixed with a shred of truth and a hint of reality.

It is not recommended that one unschooled in Kilted Sarcasm enter into a battle of the wits with a Kiltie. Going to a gunfight with a blindfold and a flyswatter will not end well for you.

(Kilted Sarcasm with Scotch is an entirely separate dialect and is wholly unintelligible to all but the most diligent students of the language.)

Kiltology #252 - Cleaning

If you happen upon a Kiltie who is cleaning something, DO NOT DISTURB HIM FOR ANY REASON!

The odds of a Kiltie cleaning of his own volition is about the same as hitting the lottery, so LEAVE HIM ALONE!! That is of course, unless you a bonnie lass with a pint, dram, or some lunch. Then do as you wish.

I am certain all of use would rather be doing anything besides cleaning.

જી છ૦

Kiltology #253 - Ringtones

When selecting a ringtone, you need to take into consideration one VERY important issue:

Your sporran will be making a hell of a lot of noise when your phone rings.

While hilarious, I don't know how many times you want your sporran to break into a rousing chorus of "I'm Too Sexy" or "Let's Get it On".

Kiltology #254 - Snow And Driving

First off, wearing a kilt does make you a better driver. You don't have to adjust every so often because the boys are getting crushed by the p@nt$.

Now, for the important part. Buying a bigger truck will NOT improve your ability to drive on snow or ice while you are talking on the phone and finish your breakfast. If you can't drive in the snow in a normal car, do NOT go buy a monster truck.

The only thing you will do is take more cars with you as you slide into the ditch and have a bigger repair bill. Not to mention it will be harder to find the lip gloss you dropped as you slid off the road.

(Can you guess what I'm worrying about?   )

CʒƧ

Kiltology #255 - Snow Shovels

When picking a snow shovel as a Kiltie, you need to be sure you do NOT buy the cheapies.

Get a real shovel, with a real handle.

It is all too easy for a Kiltie to break a lesser shovel.

(I know: I did it this morning.)

Kiltology #256 - The Sacred Throne

If a Kiltie is occupying his Sacred Throne, do not interrupt, bother, or otherwise cause him any grief. This time is the few brief moments when he can be alone with his thoughts and be at peace with the universe (unless he had bad haggis, then he is at war with it.)

Again, give the man his moment of peace and quiet. Bombard him with all sorts of calamity, noise, and chaos once he is out.

(If you have kids, read this to them every day before they go to sleep. Make them understand the sanctity of the Throne!)

CB ED

Kiltology #257 - Age And The Kilt Check

There is no age at which a woman is formally entitled to perform a kilt check of any fashion without permission.

That means just because you are 900 years old and in a wheel chair you CANNOT get someone to push you within a cane's length so you can get a peek at me kilted pride.

You will get the same reaction as everyone else does, and it will most likely not be very polite.

Kiltology #258 - Be Mindful Of Your Surroundings

It is very important to be mindful of your surroundings, especially in a difficult situation. The one thing you ignore will be your undoing.

Here is an example from life witnessed only yesterday.

A woman and her children were stuck in a store parking lot, the car unable to move.
She was trying to drive out of the ditch with no success.
Several folks came to her assistance as I came upon the scene.
The men were pushing, and she got out of the car to help get the car out of the hole.
The car came free and she promptly tried to get back in the car as it rolled away from her, children still inside.
Thirty or so feet later the car stopped as it rammed into a snowbank.
The woman, in her efforts to get in the car, fell on her face.
She got up and sat in the now-stuck car and the men again helped her out, this time she stayed in the car and was on her way.

Why is this a great example of someone not paying attention to their surroundings?

The woman left the car in gear when she got out to help push. I yelled to them that the car was in still in gear, but it was too late. The car was off, on it's way with the two children in the back seat.

(This all happened in about 20 seconds or so as I was driving into the store parking lot. I wish I had it on video.)

CꞶ℘

Kiltology #259 - Kilties

A Kiltie a day keeps the doctor away.

(P@nt$-wearing suitors, bill collectors, the bad man, and most everyone else you don't want around!)

CREDO

Kiltology #260 - Kilties And Computers

Putting Kilties and computers in the same room is a very bad idea.

A Kiltie's stubbornness, combined with his ability somehow make things work, usually ends up with some piece of computer equipment getting smashed as he tries to figure out what some p@nt$-wearing loon did and why he coded his program the way he did.

In many cases, the Kiltie simply rewrites the program or rebuilds the machine from scratch and tells the p@nt$-wearing loon to throw whatever he did in the trash.

(Yes, this is my profession; frustration abounds!)

Kiltology #261 - Kilted Humor

Have you ever noticed that most Kilties seem to be in a good mood and appear to be laughing inside about something?

It is true. They are laughing at all the guys who willingly put themselves through the torture and agony of the p@nt$ every day.

(If you happen to be in a room full of Kilties, it is because there is probably a flask or two floating around and a bonnie lass somewhere with a sheepish grin on her face.)

CRSR

Kiltology #262 - Idle Hands

Always be careful when talking to Kilties about things that need to be done. If you are not careful, you might miss that it was finished before you even had time to explain yourself!

Yes, Kilties with time on their hands always wind up doing something ... how do you think this Brotherhood came to be?

Kiltology #263 - Demolition Crews

A little known fact about Kilties is that they are the most efficient form of demolition in the known universe.

If you need a building torn down on the cheap, just tell them there is a free kilt (or single malt, depending on the crew and size of the building) coupon in the building.

It will be down in seconds.

(Just make sure the coupon is real. If you tell them and there is no coupon, you better be ready for the wrath of the Kiltie!)

CB ℰᴏ

Kiltology #264 - Power Of The Kilt

There is a group of women who hate the kilt in every way possible.

I've discovered why: The Kilt is The Great Equalizer.

It renders the powers of "Feminine Wiles" useless against the kilt wearer, effectively giving men the same alluring powers women have enjoyed since the dawn of time.

It evens the playing field on which women have dominated for far too long.

Yes, The Power of the Kilt compels you!

Kiltology #265 - Kilted Training

If you have kids, be ever vigilant in teaching them to be tolerant of those who are different from them.

It will go a long way to eliminate the kind of thoughts held by those who think the kilt is weird or immoral.

(If you have a wee boy, be VERY sure you teach him how to sweep his pleats when he sits. Chairs can be really cold if there isn't anything between you and the seat!)

൫ ൭

Kiltology #266 - Expectations

I've heard that a Kiltie can do anything. While I'm not one to counter popular opinion on this, be careful exactly how far you push this.

A single Kiltie in the woods *may* be able to build a shopping mall from a clothespin and duck tape, but don't expect the Kilts'R Us to have your tartan until at least *next* week.

Kiltology #267 - Swimming

Swimming while kilted is great fun, but you need to keep two things in mind:

1. Fish and snapping turtles are bad when swimming kilted. Be sure none are around.
2. If you see lasses with snorkels and masks getting in the water, watch your kilt. You may find yourself kilt checked from below the waves!

ೞ൫൲

Kiltology #268 - Nothing

Nothing is the most useful thing.

Kiltology #268 - Motivation

People are motivated by many things. A few things that are
sure to motivate almost any Kiltie are:

~ More kilts and kilted stuff
~ Free Kilt Inspections
~ Superbly crafted kilts and accessories
~ Free Kilt Inspections
~ Kilted gatherings over a beverage (of your choice, alcohol
or not)
~ Did I mention the Kilt Inspections?

CB 80

Kiltology #269 - Kilt Zen

He who has mastered the p@nt$, but not the kilt, will be
forever in agony.

He who has mastered the kilt, but not the p@nt$, will never
know that which he enjoys.

He who has mastered both kilt and p@nt$ shall know
boundless freedom!

Kiltology #270 - Bodhran

If you plan to give a Kiltie a bodhran, be sure to follow these steps.

1. Get a real one. A knockoff will be destroyed in days.
2. Buy a bag or two of ear plugs. Just do it, don't ask why.
3. Warn the neighbors and any friends you have who live within earshot. They will thank you.
4. Get yourself a nice, quiet place to stay at someone else's house.
5. Be patient. Remember, you bought it.
6. Introduce him to a band who practices somewhere else until he is REALLY good.
7. See #5 if you ever find yourself wanting to destroy it.
8. Consult The Wild Haggis if you are still unsure what to do. He knows.

ભ૯૦

Kiltology #271 - Kilt Night

If you ever have the opportunity to go to a kilt night, no matter where it is, GO.

You will most likely never have as much fun anywhere else as you will on a kilt night.

(If you are a bonnie lass, you may never have another opportunity to mingle with such a mass of confidence and masculinity without being surrounded by boneheaded idiots!)

Kiltology #272 - Losers

In real life there ARE winners and losers. Teaching your kids that everyone is a winner and no one is a loser gives them a much lower chance of success when competing for jobs and companions in the real world. Competition is at the heart of almost everything, taking that away from the kids will only make them children longer.

(Why do you think insurance coverage for "children" was increased to 26 years old?)

Oh ... and a word to the wise. Calling a Kiltie a loser is a bad idea. They throw trees for *fun*.

႘႘

Kiltology #273 - Bad Haggis

NEVER, under ANY circumstances, consume bad or questionable looking haggis.

It WILL do things to your insides that you only hear about in hushed voices in the dark corners of shady places.

It is the type of thing that if you had bad haggis or nothing, nothing is the desirable choice.

(So you are not confused, the effects of bad haggis are what drug companies use to gauge the effectiveness of industrial strengh laxitives before weakening them by about 90% for use in hospitals on people who are really backed up.)

Kiltology #274 - Kilted Advice

If you ever need advice on anything at all, just ask a Kiltie. It doesn't matter if he knows the answer or not, you will get some kind of advice.

DISCLAIMER: The Brotherhood of the Kilt takes no responsibility or liability on the results of implementing advice given by a Kiltie. We have no way to know if he knows what he is talking about or making it up as he goes.

(Asking what the best pair of p@nt$ to wear to a party is a bad idea. You will wind up looking like bozo or worse.)

Cฺชฺ๛๛

Kiltology #275 – Headaches

If you happen upon a Kiltie claiming to have a headache, you will need to do the following:

1. Ensure there are no people laying on the floor as if they had been beaten up.
2. Ensure the Kiltie is not incoherently mumbling to himself as if he had too much to drink.
3. Ensure there are no lasses bothering him.
4. Ensure there are no wild haggi circling him hungrily.

If any of the above applies, DO NOT APPROACH THE KILTIE. He will not be much fun to be around until he calms down.

If the above situations do not apply, then give him a couple of tylenol and a glass of water. If you have some, a bit of food would also be good.

Kiltology #276 - Being Humble

DO NOT flaunt or brag excessively about a new possession to a Kiltie, especially one who is in a foul mood.

You may wind up in the hospital having it extracted from a very uncomfortable place.

ଔଓ

Kiltology #277 - Fear

If you ever see a Kiltie running with a look of urgent fear in his eyes, GET OUT OF HIS WAY NOW!!!

He most likely had some really bad haggis and will run you over if you are in his way.

Kiltology #278 - Bombs

There is a very real reason why kilts were decreed weapons of war.

Should a Kiltie pass gas, he has the ability to trap the noxious cloud beneath his kilt and disperse it at will with a quick twist of the waist to flail the kilt about.

Yes, the "fart bomb" is a very real thing.

ᘓᘖ

Kiltology #279 - Nutella

Nutella is a godsend for those chocoholics who want a spreadable chocolaty spread for toast, sandwiches, or pretty much anything else. You can even pretend that it is almost healthy because it is a hazelnut spread.

It is NOT kilt friendly in any way. Getting Nutella out of a wool kilt is a HUGE pain in the arse, especially if it winds up getting ground in by a 4-year-old on a sugar high.

If you are going to enjoy the greater glories of Nutella, please wear a kilt apron or a non-wool kilt. You will be sorry if you don't.

Kiltology #280 - Female Viagra

There is a very good reason drug companies cannot find a version of Viagra for women.

They can't figure out how to get a kilt to work its magic in pill form.

CB ℘

Kiltology #281 - Sharks

It is well known that sharks are apex predators all around the world.

What is not so well known is that sharks are aquatic puppies for Kilties.

They know better than to try to mess with us; they just don't have to mojo to beat a Kiltie.

Kiltology #282 - Honesty

If you do not want to hear the truth, you shouldn't ask a
Kiltie his opinion.

You have a 50/50 chance of getting the truth which you
don't want to hear, IF he isn't in a feisty mood. Then you are
sure you hear it.

(Translation: Don't ask a Kiltie if those jeans make your butt
look big. If they do, you have a good chance he will tell you
as such.)

EDIT: The odds of getting told the truth can vary wildly
from Kiltie to Kiltie. 50/50 is just an average of honest
answers vs. the "right" answer becuase he is just trying to see
what the inside of those jeans looks like.

CB ED

Kiltology #283 - Wits

If you plan to enter into a battle of wits with a Kiltie, bring a
lot of friends. You will need their help.

Going alone is like going to an army tank fight with a broken
flyswatter, which I would not suggest trying.

Kiltology #284 - Flying

There is no greater kilted joy than flying while kilted. You get
excellent service from the flight staff and LOTS of attention.

That is, of course, once you get through the hell of the TSA
before boarding the plane. If you wear a kilt, you WILL get
every type of check or inspection at their disposal and maybe
even a few that have not been actually approved.

Once you get through the check, you can be sure there are
several people (some blushing the whole time) who know
more about your anatomy than you and your doctor know -
COMBINED!

CR&O

Kiltology #285 - Doubt

Never under any circumstance let a Kiltie know that you
doubt he can do something.

Come hell or high water, he will do everything in his power
to prove you wrong.

(Why do you think we know that kilts do not make good
parachutes?)

Kiltology #286 - Warmth

If any of you bonnie lasses out there feel yourself catching a chill, find yourself a Kiltie to warm up.

Here's why:

1. Traditional kilts have 8 yards of wool ...VERY warm
2. A kilt naturally traps heat beneath it. Again, VERY warm
3. Odds are, he is talking up a storm, meaning he is generating a LOT of hot air!

(Be sure to warn him if you plan to take advantage of #2.)

൪൫

Kiltology #287 - Idiot

How do you know you are the idiot?

When you try to help break up a bar fight and the guy you are pulling out of the pile works at the bar.

(yeah ... it happened ... not happy about it.)

Kiltology #288 - Watches

For the Kilties on the prowl out there (actively or otherwise)
always keep a time piece in your sporran and not on your
wrist.

Lasses asking for the time will be forced to wait while you get
your pocket watch out of your sporran, which, in itself, has
not-so-subtle suggestions about it.

It also gives her and you time to come up with more items to
discuss.

Yes, the Power of the Kilt compels you!

CB SO

Kiltology #289 - Endurance

There is no creature on Earth with the endurance of a Kiltie.

Here is a perfect example: Spend a week with your mom in
town, two sick kids, the only other guy on your work team
quits, no single malt, and only one can of Guinness
WITHOUT going completely insane.

Everyone I've heard of who has gone through such trials has
very large books written about them and this is just a normal
day for a Kiltie.

Kiltology #290 - Suggestion

The kilt is more powerful in its ability to plant subliminal suggestions than even the most powerful hypnotist or psychic.

All it takes is a single swish of the pleats and women swoon. No need for words at all.

If you want to multiply the effect exponentially, do the sporran dance for a few seconds.

(Just don't talk ... you will most likely talk yourself out of whatever you were going to get.)

☙❧

Kiltology #291 - The Boogey Man

There is an oft-forgotten bit of history regarding the Boogey Man.

He was in fact created by adults in cultures who had gone to war with kilted folks and lost.

He was far less scary than the truth ... that you NEVER mess with a man in a kilt!

Kiltology #292 - Worst Kind

The worst kind of Kiltie out there is a sick one.

Not only is he medically sick, he is most likely very cranky, irritable, and otherwise disagreeable.

Ever hear the one about not poking a sleeping bear? Well, bears have a saying.

"Don't ever go near a sick Kiltie. You will wind up on the short end of a sporran strap!"

ꅇꤗ

Kiltology #293 - Speed

If you haven't noticed, traditional Highland games do not include running or speed events.

Ever wonder why?

The only thing a Kiltie has ever had to run from is his beautiful, loving wife / girlfriend when she discovers he's been at the pub too long again!

Any man who can live through that (and not wind up living alone) has no equal in man or beast!

Kiltology #294 - Coffee

One of the easiest ways to get on the good side of many Kilties is to give them a good cup of coffee in the morning.

Just be careful. It is also the one of the fastest ways to get on their bad side if there are grounds in the bottom of the cup.

Getting a mouthful of dirt is not the way to start any day, especially after a prolonged squawk the night before!

CR ജെ

Kiltology #295 - Tired

There is no greater evil on this Earth than simply being tired.

Lack of sleep, fatigue, or whatever else you want to call it. It is just plain evil.

If you ever encounter a tired Kiltie, see Kiltology #294 before proceeding.
It just might save your life.

Kiltology #296 - Contacts

If there was ever anything that Kilties did VERY well it was generate a very lengthy list of contacts.

There are two reasons for this:

1. People naturally gravitate to a man in a kilt. They want to hang out with the cool people.
2. Anyone wearing a kilt obviously has the balls and determination to get things done. That is what people want, especially the lasses.

 C3 80

Kiltology #297 - Intelligence

It is a well known fact that the smartest man in the world wears a kilt.

If you doubt this fact, just ask the next guy in a kilt you see.

Yes, if you looked through the history of incredible innovations and invention, there are a great number of Kilties on the list.

(I know this is a direct contadiction of #235.
I got smarter.)

Kiltology #298 - Futility

It is completely futile to attempt to raise two young kids to be successful, tolerant of others, and well-mannered, while at the same time trying not to offend the sensibilities of the politically correct masses of our "polite" society.

It it were up to this Kiltie, we would dial it back about 60+ years where everyone was responsible for their own actions, had to deal with real and immediate consequences, and actually lost a real competition to someone who was more prepared than they were.

CRLSCO

Kiltology #299 - Repellent

The kilt has built-in idiot repellent.

The only idiots who dare approach a Kiltie are either drunk or have a stupid "hey, is that a kilt?" question.

I've noticed that everyone else (sales folks at kiosks at the mall or stores and the general nutjobs out there) tend to stay away.

The repellent is enhanced with either a leather jacket or a shirt that says something witty like "Guns don't kill people. I kill people." on it.

(Disclaimer: This repellent has no effect on drunk women. Proceed at your own risk)

Kiltology #300 - Fools

When playing practical jokes on people, Kilties should *never* be on the receiving end of your "humor".

These folks decided to *throw trees for fun.* Can you imagine what they can come up with to get you back for a practical joke?

You might wind up duct taped to a sheep or worse!

ԾՅՖԾ

Kiltology #301 - Eating

If you happen upon a Kiltie who is in the middle of eating, do not try to engage him in conversation until he is finished.

There are scant few times a Kiltie gets some peace a quiet. Eating is one of them.

Blathering about how your great-great-aunt twice removed was 1/124th Scottish will only get you the silent treatment as he eats.

(Or worse, depending on who the Kiltie is and when the last time he ate whatever he is trying to enjoy.)

Kiltology #302 - Worn

There is a very specific reason why the subject of "what is worn beneath a kilt" is the primary concern of many females when a Kiltie is around.

They are not checking articles of clothing, but rather the function of that which is beneath the kilt.

They assume (with good reason) that a Kiltie's prowess is well above normal, and his "Kiltie's pride" seldom goes untended. She wants to make sure it isn't "worn out".

ଓ ୫୦

Kiltology #303 - Brains

While it is well known that Kilties, as a whole, are the most brilliant folks on the planet, there is a little known dark side to this truth.

A Kiltie, in efforts to do something brilliant, has a 50/50 shot of doing the single most boneheaded thing possible, with the absolute worst outcome.

Yes ... that is why we are in so many comedy routines. With as many brilliant Kilties, there are an equal number of complete blockheads.

Kiltology #304 - Philosophy

Every Kiltie is born a Stand-Up Philosopher.

If you ask most any Kiltie the most intellectually stimulating question you can imagine, you will be graced with a very lengthy discourse on how the answer to that question is a direct result of something he did as a young kilted man while drinking a Guinness and fending off a raging horde of snow haggi with only his kilt pin as a weapon!

ෲ

Kiltology #305 - Planning

When dealing with any issue that requires intricate planning and detail, asking a Kiltie to explain it to you while he is working isn't a good idea.

By the time you understand what he is talking about, odds are, he could have already finished what he is working on.

(If you ask after, you will probably get an answer like "I dunno, I just did it".)

See Kiltology #303 and #297 for reference.

You can also see Kiltology #304 if you think it was easy for him.

Kiltology # 306 - Control

If you are going to relinquish control of ANYTHING to a Kiltie, be EXTREMELY specific as to what new power this control conveys.

If you are not VERY specific, it should not be a surprise if the Kiltie conquers a country, takes over a business, or builds a shopping mall if you just asked him to watch the dog without any further instruction.

CB&

Kiltology #307 - Giggles

The Giggle is one of the most feared sounds in all of kiltdom.

A quiet giggle is the telltale warning that the Kiltie is about to be attacked by the most crafty and devious of hunters: the kilt-loving lass.

These sly beasties will stop at nothing to claim their prize ... a glimpse up the kilt!

(In some cases, they go one step further and move in for tactile verification of their visual findings!)

Kiltology #308 - Taxes

Bothering a Kiltie deep in thought regarding the issue of taxes is a bad idea.

Odds are, he is trying to solve world hunger, figure out the cure for cancer, or find the famous never-ending pint.

He will most like respond with an economy-saving tax plan which will, of course, be completely ignored, thereby making him rather grumpy for bothering him.

(Moral of the story: If you don't want to listen to what he has to say, don't ask!)

C03 80

Kiltology #309 - Odd Food

If you happen upon a Kiltie who is eating something you have never seen before, DO NOT ask him about it until he is done eating it.

He wears a kilt. It is most likely that he knows of and eats food that you can't get at a fast food place. Let him eat in peace.

(This is especially true if he is eating a good scotch egg, boxty or haggis. Good ones are hard to find in most places, and he just might remind you how rude it is to bother someone eating such fine foods. It could hurt.)

Kiltology #310 - Determination

There is not a living creature on this Earth more determined
than a Kiltie with his mind set on something.

There is no mountain he can't move nor sea he can't cross to
accomplish his goal.

(That is, of course, unless he is swayed by a bonnie lass with
a wink and a grin. His task can wait an hour or two.)

CB ℘

Kiltology #311 - Demands

Demands are things you just don't give to a Kiltie.

Think about it. He is in a kilt. Do you really think it wise to
try to boss him around?

(Be careful ... he might turn rapidly, unleashing THIS (see
Kiltology #278) upon you!)

Kiltology #312 - Competition

In any competition, do not underestimate the calm Kiltie.
His presence alone will give him an advantage over the
bifurcated. They will be curious, confused, or simply
ignorant of his kilted nature.

Having the stones to show up kilted in itself will cause a good
amount of respect for him. Not knowing what he is capable
of will be a cause for concern among most of the rest.

Not knowing if he is regimental or not, and the fear of
finding out the hard way, will keep all but the most confident
of opponents at bay.

CB ঠ০

Kiltology #314 - Rain

If you see a Kiltie dancing around in the rain wearing nothing
but his kilt, leave him be.

He is washing his kilt. It is really hard to wash a kilt at the
local laundromat if you haven't anything else to wear!

Kiltology #315 - Glass Walls

It is a little known fact that glass walls on escalators are NOT being covered for the 'privacy' of lasses, but to eliminate crowds of randy lasses from gathering beneath the escalators in malls where Kilties are known to roam.

Trying to control a crowd of lasses with a Kiltie on an escalator is not something easily accomplished ... even with cattle prods!

ᏸ ᏉᎥ

Kiltology #316 - Rocks

Do you know how you can tell male rocks from female rocks?

Female rocks will get in the way and trip a Kiltie just to get a glimpse of his kilted pride.

Male rocks are those noises you hear when out hiking. They are getting out of the way. They don't want the Kiltie to pick them up and throw them around.

Kiltology #317 - Dancing

Ever wonder why a lass dancing with a Kiltie always has her hands down by her sides?

It is much easier to do a kilt check while dancing if her hands are ALWAYS at her sides!

CB ഇ

Kiltology #318 - Hunting

It is a little known fact that the Kilt is one of the few weapons of war still used for hunting.

Just ask any lass at the pub, a kilt is the most valuable and dangerous weapon in any Kiltie's arsenal. If you are lucky, she will show you why.

[Insert filthy joke here]

Kiltology #319 - Morale

If you ever are in need of drastic measures to increase morale, be it at work, play, or you are simply having a rough day:

Go find a Kiltie and invite him to join you and your group of friends/co-workers/drinking buddies.

Morale will raise faster than a sporran at a kilt-checking competition!

C

Kiltology #320 - Kilt Washing

The proper washing of a kilt is a time consuming process, needing careful attention and concentration so the kilt itself is not damaged.

It is also best not to wash one's kilt in public. You will be stared at by almost everyone (including some blushing lasses) and just might wind up in jail for letting your Kiltie's pride get some sun.

Kiltology #321 - Coffee

If offering a Kiltie a cup of coffee, for the love of all that is kilted, make sure it is not burnt!

If he wanted to drink something foul, wretched, and disgusting, he could just wring out his kilt into a cup after a rainstorm and drink that.

(FYI, please don't try it ... not something I would suggest)

CB ED

Kiltology #322 – Pick Up Lines

Kilties have no use for pick up lines when talking to women.

Why spew cheesy BS when the kilt will break the ice for you?

Kiltology #323 - Motivation

When seeking motivational advise from a Kiltie, be sure you have no valuables or hard objects in your back pockets.

Cell phones and other such devices don't react well to boots at high velocity.

ᬛᬺ

Kiltology #324 - Skilled Labor

If you happen upon a Kiltie working a trade or skilled labor, do NOT for one second consider him a failure for not having a desk job.

He has a far less chance of losing his job to some over seas company who pays only a few dollars an hour and odds are his education debt is a lot less than yours.

Kiltology #325 - Pain

Pain can be defined as a new tattoo being discovered by your five-year-old child.

This also happens to be the same time she discovers both drumsticks and velcro.

CB ❧

Kiltology #326 - Metaphor

When preparing for a discussion with a Kiltie, you must be ready to handle metaphor translation very quickly.

It is a hell of a lot easier to explain the complexities of existence as a box of chocolates, instead of going into the vagaries of the metaphysical and mythological, ESPECIALLY if there is single malt involved!

Kiltology #327 - Trouble

There are exactly two kinds of trouble Kilties get into.

Type 1. He winds up in jail or the hospital for being "that guy".

Type 2. He winds up in the hospital or jail after a brief "meeting" with the father of the bonnie lass he met last night at the pub.

If a Kiltie is doing anything else, odds are it is little more than him practicing his trade as a standup philosopher.

CﬤƧ

Kiltology #328 - Fair

Fair is a place you go to have fun and play William Wallace or She-Ra.

Fair isn't what you see in the morning or have to deal with every day.

Asking for fair is like asking for a winning lottery ticket. Everyone wants it, painfully few get it.

Kiltology #329 - Power Tools

It is a little know fact that power tools were actually invented to compete with Kilted workers.

One Kiltie with his bare hands could do as much work as a dozen p@nt$-clad laborers.

(They also drastically reduced work site injuries as the lasses passing by weren't interested in the laborers without kilts who were using power tools and stopped having 'wardrobe malfunctions' to get the Kiltie's attention.)

03 80

Kiltology #331 - Early

Early is that time before you can safely approach a Kiltie.

If you encounter one, you will know you are early almost instantly, as he may very well turn into a fire-breathing spawn of the damned who is hell-bent on your complete and total decimation because you showed up before he has finished his morning coffee.

Kiltology #332 - Frustration

Frustration is defined as trying to recoil a chainsaw rope spring by hand with two hyper kids running around the house as the Red Sox are not winning the game.

(The rope spring has a hook on the end that would easily tear my kilt a new one were it to slip and catch a thread.)

CB8O

Kiltology #333 - Elation

Elation is getting a damn chainsaw rope spring recoiled by hand without ripping my kilt or skin to shreds, while the Sox are in first place and the Bruins are going to the Stanley Cup Finals!

(Took four hours to get the @#$^%@#$^% spring in.)

Kiltology #334 - Ninja

There are three tell tale signs you have been assaulted by a
Kilted Ninja:

1. There is no single malt to be found.
2. All the p@nt$ have been destroyed.
3. Every bonnie lass within 50 yards of the "attack" is
blushing and grinning from ear to ear.

&

Kiltology #335 - P@nt$

In the eyes of every Kiltie, p@nt$ are the devil incarnate. A
new pair of these insidious creations make Satan himself
seem like a puppy napping in a pile of feathers under the
moonlight.

They are evil, pure and simple. Avoid them at all costs.

Your best defense against a rather persistent pair of p@nt$ is
fire and something very pointy and sharp.

Kiltology #336 - Lasses

There ne'er was beheld a greater sight than a bonnie lass in a mini-kilt.

Except, of course, TWO bonnie lasses in mini-kilts!

CB SO

Kiltology #338 - 6:30 Am

6:30 am is a glorious time to be awake. The birds chirping, the dew glistening on the grass, the sun peeking over the treetops. Bunnies scurrying around to eat before anything bigger wakes up.

Unless, of course, you are not awake to enjoy nature's beauty, but to figure out why on Earth your kids are screaming at the top of their lungs to get out of bed and play.

The kilt has no power over this. We Kilties have to suck it up and deal with it ... with a healthy dose of hi-test coffee, of course.

Kiltology #339 - Wiping

As a traditional Kiltie, proper wiping is of the utmost importance.

You never know where you are going to sit next ... or the impact your lack of attention may have on those around you.

CʒƧ

Kiltology #340 - Rain

Rain Sucks. Even in your best, most invincible kilt, rain sucks.

It sucks most in the Berkshires during a torrential downpour, late at night, and you are trying to keep the meager fire from going out so the 50+ kids entrusted to your care have something to keep the creepy crawlies away.

Did I also mention that the only flashlight I had was lost ... so it sucked super wicked bad, as Quinn might say.

Kiltology #341 - Mosquitos

Mosquitoes up the kilt is the single worst experience a Kiltie can have.

If you don't wear a kilt ... just take my word for it. If you do wear one, I'm sorry for that pain you just had in your stomach.

ಲ೫ಬಿ

Kiltology #342 - Hot

There isn't a kilt on Earth which can help protect you from the vicous heat and humidity of an Oklahoma summer.

Your best bet is to just get a casual kilt and sit at home in front of a fan like a dog would.

Kiltology #343 - Sunrise

Watching the sunrise can be a wonderfully beautiful thing. The sun slowly peeks up over the horizon, the squirrels playing in the damp grass, and the birds chirping away as if to say "Good Morning!"

That is, of course, unless you are abruptly and most unceremoniously woken up by an airborne 4-year-old trying to practice the some flying attack he saw on a superhero show. A flying elbow to the sporran when a sporran is not being worn is NOT the recommended method of waking a Kiltie!

CB&O

Kiltology #344 - Lucidity

Lucidity, defined as "characterized by clear perception or understanding; rational or sane" by Dictionary.com.

If you wake any Kiltie at 4:00 am expecting any form of lucidity, you are completely out of your gourd. You will need to give the poor guy at least half an hour and a cup of coffee before expecting any kind of sane or rational response.

If you don't provide coffee and time, you are most likely going to receive a guttural, angry growl and possibly some kind of bedside projectile at high speed.

Kiltology #345 - Convenience Stores

Convenience stores are possibly the greatest thing ever.

The only major downfall with all convenience stores is that they are not designed for Kilties. Every time I am in one with a kilt on, there seems to be a serious increase in people congregating as they all try to look like they are not looking at the kilt. They all are running into things, bumping into each other, and generally losing all sense of where they are or what they are doing.

On the other hand, it is kinda funny to walk in and see the chaos ensue. Like shaking up an ant farm and then dropping a sugar cube in the middle.

CB&O

Kiltology #346 - Lawn Gnomes

It is a little known fact that Lawn Gnomes were invented by a bonnie Scottish lass.

They were placed in lawns the world over with tiny cameras built in to catch a glimpse up the Kiltie's kilt for the lass to enjoy later.

(It was many years later when the lass innovated further with the invention of the wifi video camera, making the lawn gnome far more effective.)

Kiltology #347 - Fireworks

It is a little known fact that fireworks were actually created by accident by a bonnie Scottish lass trying to look up a Kiltie's kilt whilst he slept.

The lass created what is currently known as a sparkler with a little too much black powder and wound up burning very large holes in the front aprons. The gent woke with such a start that he kicked the sparkler into the lass's box of sparklers and the first fireworks show was underway!

(The Kiltie and lass eventually did get married and had a great many children. Rumor has it the lass had to apologize for burning the kilt MANY times.)

☙❧

Kiltology #348 - The Grin

Every Kiltie knows "The Grin".

It is that silly, coy smirk and blush on the face of almost every woman who is curious about what is being worn under the kilt. It is very obvious, and in many cases completely involuntary.

It is most easily identified by making eye contact with said woman. When she realizes you know she is staring and grinning, she generally does something completely odd, like walk into a wall, trip over herself, or start to incoherently babble into the wrong side of her phone. It is quite humorous.

Kiltology #349 - Blame

Blame is used when someone would rather just complain and avoid responsibility instead of figuring out what the problem is and trying to correct it.

So, based on that, BLAME is Bulls*** Lame-A$$ Moronic Excuses.

It is in your best interest not to blame a Kiltie for much. It will most likely not be good for you in the end.

 CB ℰᴐ

Kiltology #350 - Invasion

There is a very good reason aliens have never successfully invaded since the advent of the Kilt.

They didn't want to have to go back home telling their buddies they got their butts kicked by aliens in skirts!

Kiltology #351 - Curiosity

It is a well known saying that "Curiosity Killed the Cat"

The only thing curiosity ever did for a Kiltie was get him on the business end of many curious lass's father's shovels, pitchforks, or other implement of retribution.

Worst part of this situation is the Kiltie wasn't the curious one!!!

CꝪ℘

Kiltology #352 - Love

True love is when someone cares for another so much he put his love's needs ahead of his own.

A Kiltie in love is a force to be reckoned with. A regular Kiltie can defeat whole armies by himself. Give him someone he loves to defend and nothing will stand in their way!

(If you have the stones to question this, just ask any Kiltie if you can dance with his date.)

Kiltology #353 - Donuts

It is a little known fact that donuts were actually invented by Scottish lasses.

They learned that they could make these delicious treats very easily and feed them to Kilties. The Kilties are then slowed down dramatically after eating a few, making it far easier for the lasses to catch their elusive prey.

Of course, it backfired on the lasses, as some of the Kilties enjoyed so many donuts they had little desire do much else but sit around.

Modern lasses now spend more time trying to motivate their Kilties to get off the couch instead of giving them the sport of the chase.

ဆ႘ဆ

Kiltology #354 - Sunburn

One of a Kiltie's worst nightmares is to wake up with a sunburn in the middle of his back. He can't reach it, can't lay down, can't really sit comfortably anywhere, and can't do much of anything that would require any contact with his back without inflicting pain upon himself.

The only thing more frightening than the sunburn is the lasses who don't know about the sunburn. As they flock to the Kiltie, they will unwittingly cause him pain over and over as they give in to the Power of the Kilt, their innate powers over men failing completely.

Kiltology #355 - Challenge

If you want to challenge a Kiltie, please think about what you are asking. Be certain your request is an actual challenge.

Think of some of the things done by Kiltie..

~ Successfully defeated all wielding the Power of the P
~ Conquered entire countries and communities of non-Kilties
~ Drained many a pub and eatery of all their provisions

So ... if you want to give a serious challenge, think of something like world peace, free energy, or the end of that #$%^@#$% dancing purple dinosaur!

ოჳ ჶე

Kiltology #356 - Thank You
The most powerful words that can ever been said are not "I love you" or "F*** You" or some conglomeration of filth and putridity that even I cannot utter in my foulest of moods.

They are "Thank You".

A simple "Thank You" said honestly can mean more to a person than hitting the lottery (or whatever great thing you can imagine).

Sincere gratitude is something, we as a society, are seriously lacking these days. Tell those you appreciate "Thank You" once and a while, you will be surprised the response you get.

(Be warned ... a Kiltie's gratitude, once earned, is very hard to get away from.)

Kiltology #357 - Conversation

The best way for any businessman to successfully find and keep his customers is to be willing to talk to his current and future customers ... a LOT.

For Kilties, this is second nature even on a bad day. A wee dram and some pub fare can lead to conversations spanning months or more on every topic imaginable (and some best left unmentioned!)

(Be careful with the drams ... the more drams in, the more colorful the conversation coming out!)

ᢒᘔᘓᢙ

Kiltology #358 - Socks

When deciding your attire for the day, you cannot be too cautious on what socks or kilt hose you wear.

Why? Shoes and socks are all the clothing many Kilties wear under the kilt, so you should be certain you are wearing the ones that will get you the most attention if that is what you are looking for. You could always go barefoot and answer the question with "Nothing, I'm barefoot all the time!"

Kiltology #359 - The Pot

If you are going to fill it, then fill it.

Otherwise, get the hell out of the way. I had too much single malt, Guinness, and bad haggis last night.

CƷՑƆ

Kiltology #360 – 7th Sense

It is well known that can people have a sixth sense, seemingly knowing when someone else is around or other premonitions.

What is NOT well known, but proven daily, is that Kilties have a 7th Sense - Mind Control!

With this ability of mind control, a skilled Kiltie can attract countless females who normally would have nothing to do with him. This power also enables him to distract people from almost anything, to be omniscient (based on the number of questions Kilties are asked by random people vs. everyone else), to have McGyver-like repair skills and to control large crowds with a few words.

(Don't mistake any of these with the power of the Drunken Kiltie. They look the same, except the Drunken Kiltie will eat your food, drink your whiskey and beer, search for your cousin, sleep on your couch, and expect you to go to breakfast with him the next morning! This will also be amazing, though, because it will seem the Kiltie has avoided ALL ill effects of the alcohol!)

Kiltology #361 - Brooding

If you happen upon a Kiltie who seems to be stewing in his
mind or generally detached from his immediate surrounding,
be VERY careful how you approach him if you decide to
offer a kind ear. He most likely has some very heavy issues
he is trying to sort through, so do not be upset or angered if
he isn't his normal jovial self.

Be sure to to hear him out if he offers, and let him be if he
does not. Forcing yourself into his world will not be good
for you.

CB ⅏

Kiltology #362 - Real Men Don't Wear Kilts

For the non-Kilties out there:

Before you decide to make fun of a man in a kilt, or skirt as
you would call it to get a laugh, because "real men don't wear
skirts" think of this:

How many pictures of Jesus Christ, or major figures in almost
any other faith out there, have you seen wearing p@nt$?

Think first, then speak, else you become the butt of your own
joke.

Kiltology #363 - Blind Eye

Before wasting your time poking fun at the weirdo in a skirt, look in the mirror.

Turning a blind eye to your own issues is a bad idea in this case, especially if you happen to be in a pub full of Kilties!

It could be compared to walking to a gunfight with a blindfold and a broken rubber band.

 CRORO

Kiltology #364 - Strength

The wearing of a kilt, or skirt as some would call it, does not make one weak.

Not only does the Kiltie need the fortitude to deal with idiots and naysayers, some have the strength to throw trees and very large stones.

(Make sure you aren't behind a tree throwing Kiltie after he has had his haggis. If the back of his kilt flies up for no good reason, you should run!)

Kiltology #365 - Long Day

You know it is going to be a VERY long day when your two-year-old follows you around yelling, "I want tickle" for hours on end.

(This necessitates the wearing of a utility kilt, no sporran, and undergarments for the safety of all involved!)

ॐ ੬ॐ

Kiltology #366 - Underwear Day

Today apparently is "National Underwear Day".

Such a silly notion, celebrating such a useless garment. It's like trying to celebrate "p@nt$ that are too small day".

Seriously, who would celebrate something that is restrictive, awkward, and in the way all the time?

Kiltology #367 - Smile

A smile is what you have when you are happy.

A smile is given to a friend you haven't seen in a while.

A smile is on the face of children when they get ice cream.

A smile is what you see on almost every bonnie lass when she sees a Kiltie.

Some lasses even blush (and I'm sure you know why).

CঙЪ

Kiltology #368 - Clotheslines

It is a little known fact that the clothesline was NOT invented simply to dry clothes.

A few blushing bonnie lasses convinced an unsuspecting Kiltie it was far easier to air out and dry his kilt than laying it out on a rock.

Yes, the lasses were hiding in the bushes as he hung his kilt on the line the first time (and almost every time after that as well.)

Kiltology #369 - Clothes Make the Man

"Clothes make the man" is a popular phrase used by those trying to force a certain style and degree of clothedness.
Have you ever seen clothing make anything except a pile on the floor? I've not.
If clothing WERE to make a man, we all know the kilt would be doing the work.
This guy would make Superman look like a half-mashed string bean with no guts. Women the world over would abandon all their celebrity crushes and fantasies, replacing them all with this man made by the Kilt. The most interesting man in the world would beg to hang out with this guy. Fabio would relinquish his throne as king of romance novel covers.

(It is rumored that Chuck Norris was made by a group of kilts trying to prove this point, but they have not come forward to claim their victory.)

CʒꝪꝪꝪ

Kiltology #370 – Kiltface

Being kiltfaced is REALLY bad.

It means your kilt is flying up over your face.
Either you are falling VERY rapidly or someone has a powerful leafblower stuck up your kilt.
Both situations usually end badly, especially if the leafblower gets too close.
(There ARE other reasons you may become kiltfaced, but they cannot be discussed amongst polite company.)

Kiltology # 371 - P@nt$

It is a little known fact that p@nt$ were, in fact, invented by kilt-wearing peoples.

When a criminal was convicted and sent to prison they were forced to wear p@nt$ in prison, truly robbing them of EVERY freedom!

ଓଃ୨୦

Kiltology #372 - Pay Raise

If a Man in a Kilt is a man and a half, where is my 50% pay raise?

Kiltology #373 - ...and A Half

What the kilt enables us to do as "men and a half":

~ 50% more attractive.
~ 50% higher chance of being right, no matter the question.
~ 50% higher chance of knowing exactly what tickles your fancy.
~ 50% less likelihood of being stopped and bothered by random strangers begging for money.
~ 50% (or higher) chance of being able to accurately guess the correct bra size of any women within view.
~ 50% higher chance of being the object of a jealous boyfriend's rage.
~ 50% higher chance of being able to fix whatever is busted without the proper tools.
~ 50% higher chance of being the life of the party, no matter what kind of party it is.
~ 50% higher chance of dancing with the bride before the groom at their wedding.
~ 500% higher chance of getting in trouble with your significant other over any and all items in this list.

CʒꙄꙄꙄ

Kiltology #374 - Means

It is well known that, in general, we are living beyond our
means or dealing with the results of trying to do
so in the past.
Here is a helpful hint to prevent getting yourself in
a financial hole.

Buy a kilt.

One kilt will last many years, eliminating the need to buy
many pairs of short-lived p@nt$. This will save you plenty of
money over the long run with which you can help eliminate
other financial woes.
One word of caution: Kilting is known to be addictive.
Please seek out support groups if you find yourself wanting
more and more kilts, no matter how many you already have.
The Brotherhood of the Kilt offers such support.

CB&

Kiltology #375 – Bathing

When trying to determine where that smell is coming from,
this is how you can tell if the Kiltie standing next to you is the
source of the foul stench.
If you engage said Kiltie in any manner of discourse and his
kilt enters into the conversation with an intelligent comment,
you know it has been WAY too long since it has seen the
inside of anything used to wash clothes.
Be careful, arguments between a Kiltie and his kilt have been
known to happen, and they are epically dramatic, though you
will never see it on YouTube.
(Normally one of the involved parties gets pissed off and
leaves the vicinity.)

Kiltology #376 - Badass

You are, by definition, a badass if you are wearing kilt.

No point in arguing, it is a simple statement of fact.

No amount of tattoos, scars, chains, or attitude will make
someone in p@nt$ more badass than a guy in a kilt.

Accept your badassness and move on.

(Military and First Responders doubly so, even without the
kilt!)

CallBD

Kiltology #377 - Vehicles

Never ever ever judge a Kiltie by his mode of transportation.
Some have massive trucks, others ride a bicycle, and others
simply walk ... all for their own reasons.

I feel for the poor soul who deems it necessary to deride or
belittle a Kiltie based on his choice of transportation. If said
person makes it through the few moments after his oral
swashbuckling is concluded with his skull intact (due to his
luck in encountering a non-aggressive Kiltie), karma is a
beyotch.

Kiltology #378 - Waiting

If you ever think about getting your way with a Kiltie by simply trying to out wait him, you have already lost.

Kitlies are known the world over for not only being extremely determined, they can sometimes be a little hard headed.

Odds are, the Kiltie you are trying to wait out will simply out wait you just because he can.

(This is entirely a bad idea. If it turns into a lengthy event he may get agitated ... which is a whole other problem.)

 CƐ SO

Kiltology #379 - Wits

Entering a battle of wits with a Kiltie is like trying to push a rope uphill. It is the unwritten classic blunder, third under, "never get involved in a land war in Asia" and "Never go against a Sicilian when death is on the line".

Unless you are immune to viscous tongue lashings and brutal assaults on your mental faculties, I'd suggest avoiding such battles altogether.

(If you didn't already know, those are quotes from The Princess Bride.)

Kiltology #380 - Butting Heads

Don't bother butting heads with a Kiltie, figuratively or realistically.

You would have a better time ramming your head into a granite wall. It is softer.

ೞೞ

Kiltology #381 - Clean

Discussing levels of clothing cleanliness with a Kiltie is a really good way to waste a lot of your time.

The average kilt can go months or longer without a proper washing and look like they just came off the loom with very little effort.

Some more robust kilts are damn near impervious to all forms of filth and need little more than a hose off to get them clean.

One more reason kilts are superior to p@nt$ ... gotta wash your p@nt$ regularly or they look like someone washed a port-a-john with them!

Kiltology #382 Asking

If you want something done, ask a Kiltie once, give him some time and ask again if it isn't done. Do not ask every two seconds. The more often you ask in a short time, the less likely you are to get any results.

This goes doubly if it is early in the day.

⠀⠀⠀⠀⠀⠀⠀Cʒℰↄ

Kiltology #383 - Birthday Shopping

For the love of all that is holy, please do not demand a Kiltie go shopping for gifts for a little girl's birthday party.

There is exactly NOTHING he can purchase that does NOT make him feel like some kind of wierdo.

(I just did it ... damn near impossible.)

EDIT: This was NOT my daughter. Neighbor's kid turned 4 today.

Kiltology #384 - Sheep

There are great many reasons Kilties love sheep.

~ Our kilts themselves come from sheep's wool.
~ Haggis is made from sheep.
~ Tending them offers employment to many Kilties.

Best of all, it completely relieves p@nt$-wearing loons of the need for creativity when trying to insult us. They simply say, most anything ending in "with sheep" and a laugh is assured…

… So is a witty retort from the Kiltie of such strength I dare not even speak of it here.

ॐ

Kiltology #385 - Kiltie Instructions

When giving instructions to a Kiltie, no matter how simple or common you may think they are, be as explicit as possible.
If you have a specific result you are looking for and you are not precise in your instructions, you will probably not get what you expected.
The level of creativity and ability to do the amazing with nothing will most likely kick in if there is ANY question as to what is required.
If you say "build me a shed over there" without specifics, it is more likely you will get a shed big enough and well-enough appointed to house your entire family. Far more than just four walls, a roof, some doors and things to hang your tools.

If your Kiltie is extremely gifted, there is no limit as to what might happen.

Kiltology #386 - For Granted

Never, EVER start taking a Kiltie's kindness and generosity for granted. You have obviously gotten on his good side. You want to stay there.

Taking a Kiltie for granted and getting pissed when he stops being nice or doing whatever it is you like is a sure-fire way to REALLY piss him off.

You don't want that.

CB&O

Kiltology #387 - Leafblowers

It is a little known fact that the leafblower was actually invented by bored Scottish lasses.

A few of them were sitting on a bench and saw a Kiltie walk over one of those steam exhaust grates in the city and had a whole lot of dirty thoughts go through their head.

The next day, after spending hours sitting on that same bench, they figured out how to stick a pipe on a portable fan and started chasing Kilties on the spot!

The rest, as they say, is history.

Kiltology #388 - Repetition

Repetition is one of the most effective forms of learning.
- Repeating a task helps commit it to memory, making it easier to execute in the future.
- Repeating a phrase makes it easier to say in the future.
- Being made fun of for wearing the kilt repeatedly makes it far easier to rebut the insult with wit and confidence, especially if the offending party is wearing p@nt$!

❧

Kiltology #389 - Balls Out

It is a well documented fact that most men will go balls out most of their lives if given the chance.
What is not well documented is the fact that Kilties have the ability to go balls out for far greater lengths of time than any other types of man.
In warmer climates Kilties can go balls out for very long periods of time.
In colder climates Kilties can still go balls out longer than regular folks, although cold is cold no matter what you are wearing.
Word of warning: Attempting to go balls out all the time has been proven to be extremely dangerous and has landed many a gent in the hospital.
Be wary when going balls out for too long!

(For those who don't know, a friend explained to me that old steam engines had a governor rod with ball shaped spinning weights on the ends. When the engine was running at maximum speed, centrifugal force moved the balls all the way out, or "balls out" ... also means to go like hell.)

Kiltology #390 - Aroma

It is well known that Kilties are strong and skilled at a great many things.
Knowing that, you should not be surprised or shocked should the aroma from a restroom recently occupied by a Kiltie jump out at you and physically knocks you on your backside.

If you happened to have spent the previous night in a pub with said Kiltie, you are taking your life into your hands. I've seen hazmat teams called for lesser disasters.

ᘓᘔᘓ

Kiltology #391 – Balloons

It is a little known fact that balloons were invented by sly Scottish lasses.

They would quietly pin one to the back of a kilt in hopes that it would rise to the sky, taking the kilt with it.
Eventually this project became legitimate research backed by several women's groups. It took a lot of trial and error before they found the proper balloon size, which of course, is now used as weather balloons to better detect and track natural updrafts in and around Scotland and other kilted locations.

(As you can imagine, these lasses spent a LOT of time on research and did not have to be very sneaky about it. They brought scotch with them on every research trip to ensure there were plenty of research 'subjects' willing to be 'experimented' upon.)

Kiltology #392 - Politically Correct

For the love of all that is haggis, please do not get into an
argument with a Kiltie about political correctness.
The very concept of being politically correct in the presence
of Kilties is like sailing a boat with a screen door bottom.
Total waste of time doomed to epic failure from the start.
Who in his right mind talks to a man wearing a kilt (which is
by definition a man's skirt) about being cautious of the
sensitivities of those around him, especially at the pub? I've
not met a Kiltie who has NOT been the butt of insanely
degrading and derogatory insults from the mouths of those
very same people espousing a need for politically correct
speech and behavior.

(This happened to me last week ... epic fail is an
understatement!)

⅌

Kiltology #393 - Control

The theory of control over another human being is, at best, a
pipe dream, at worst a painful exercise in futility.

Control over another must be granted by the person who is
to be controlled. There is always a way to avoid control,
although it might not be a good option.
If you don't believe me, just stop by to watch my kids for a
few hours. They will show you exactly how futile it is to try to
exercise control over those who do not want to be controlled,
especially if they have friends over.

Kiltology #394 - Persistance

There is no force on this Earth more persistant than a Kiltie on a mission.

That is, except for a 2-year-old girl who knows you have brownies hidden somewhere and she REALLY wants them.

CB ℰↃ

Kiltology #395 - Velcro

It is a little known fact that velcro was invented by kilt-wearing Scotsman.

Before velcro, and the noise it makes when separating the two sides, young Scottish lasses would sneak up on unsuspecting Kilties standing at the bar and tie the laces of their brogues together. They would then sneak off and wait until the unfortunate soul went kilt over keister and fell to the floor, exposing his kilted pride for the world to see.

Velcro's distinct noise put an end to this for all but the most determined lasses. It is rumored one young lass velcro'd an entire pipe band's shoes to each other one evening after a parade. The entire band did fall over at once, but the identity of the lass is still unknown to this day.

Kiltology #396 - In A Sporran

You should never ever ask a Kiltie what is in his sporran.

He just might show you.

CR SO

Kiltology #397 - Why Wear A Sporran

Contrary to popular belief, a sporran is worn for a great many more reasons than just to hold the coin and flask.

It is perfect protection from:

~ The foot of the wife / girlfriend when getting home after staying at the pub too long.
~ The foot of the wife / girlfriend if she sees a bonnie lass looking at you in your kilt.
~ The foot of the wife / girlfriend if you look at a bonnie lass.
~ The foot of the wife / girlfriend if there are any women around at all.
~ The head and shoulders of kids who are not paying attention to where they are running.
~ The foot of the wife / girlfriend if she is in a bad mood.
~ The foot of the wife / girlfriend if the wind is blowing the wrong way.
~ The foot of the wife / girlfriend if she thinks you think she looks fat in whatever she is wearing.
~ The foot of the wife AND girlfriend if they happen to meet each other.

Kiltology #399 - New Realities Of Fatherhood

As we Kilties grow from children to adults to parents, there are a great many realities we must accept with the role of guardian and father to our offspring.

~ Privacy, of any kind - gone. Kids WILL find you no matter where you go to hide.

~ Personal space - that bubble of space around your body you once enjoyed is popped. If the kids could climb into your shoes they would.

~ Sleep - gone. You will be woken up at the wost possible times ... over and over again.

~ Quiet time – again, gone. The only time they are quiet is when they are asleep, which is when you sleep.

~ Cleanliness - gone. The concept that if you clean something it will stay clean is no more. If it stays clean for more than a few hours you have scored a victory.

~ TV time - this is also shot, as kids shouldn't be watching grown-up TV shows and movies. Last thing you need is your 5-year-old son running around saying "Giggity". The exception is when the game is on. No fool in a costume singing and jumping around like a loon is taking away my Red Sox!

~ Work time. We all have loads of things to do that cannot be done while watching kids. It takes extensive planning and large quantities of wine/beer to convince neighbors and friends to watch the kids while you fix the hole in the roof or repair the fence that fell over a year ago.

~ Regimental - it is a bad idea to go au-naturale when around loads of kids, especially in sue-happy countries.

The biggest change is your availability to go hang out with friends. Totally shot all to hell. It takes more planning than to fix that fence, and has a far higher rate of "falling through" as whomever is supposed to watch the kids knows you are just going to hang out and there is nothing being fixed or improved upon at the house.

Kiltology #400 - Kilted Fatherhood

You know you have reached complete fatherhood when you see a sweet deal on a limited-issue kilt and the first thing you think of is how many boxes of diapers or gallons of milk that money could buy...

...and do not buy the kilt.

☙❦❧

Kiltology #401 - The Hardest Part

The hardest part of wearing the kilt for the first time has almost nothing to do with the act of putting on the kilt.

The hardest part is taking that first step out your front door when you proclaim to the world that you are a Kiltie, and dealing with the world's response.

(Dealing with groups of teenagers in public is the first major test of a new Kiltie's mettle. A well-honed wit usually makes quick work of the situation, but it can be very difficult for the unprepared.)

Kiltology #402 - The Kilted Mind

Don't even bother trying to figure out the mind of a Kiltie.

There is more going on in there than your average college classroom.

(If you don't believe it, just take a Kiltie with you to a college classroom. I'm sure he will take it over in a few seconds or less.)

CR&O

Kiltology #403 - I Love You

Nothing says "I Love You" like a Kiltie on his hands and knees trying to remove some unknown funk from the kitchen tiles.

(Be sure you don't approach from the back. You might get a whole lot more love than you bargained for!)

Kiltology #404 - Creativity

Creativity can be defined as a Kiltie finding ways to entertain a six-year-old boy and three-year-old girl in a place devoid of inexpensive playtime options with a daytime high over 100° F in the shade for weeks at a time, getting them to bed without a catastrophic meltdown, OR bribing them with toys and candy.

ॐ ॐ

Kiltology #405 - Joy

You will most likely never see such joy on a woman's face as when she performs her first kilt check on a properly dressed Kiltie!

Kiltology #406 - Your Horrible Day

When you feel like hell, have a million people nagging you to do stuff, your head is killing you, and it seems like the world is falling all around you, remember this:

Somewhere a guy is having a far worse day than you simply becuase he is sweating his smothered manhood off in his p@nt$!

Kiltology #407 - Make It Happen

One kilted quality I've seen in a majority of my brethren is this:

Kilties are busy doing while everyone else is whining about how much they have to do, or how hard life is.

Expecting sympathy from a Kiltie while whining about how difficult your life is has the same result as going to a gun fight with a wet noodle and a blindfold...

...and you can't find your noodle.

Kiltology #408 - Appreciation

Appreciate your friends, family, and those you care for.

It will be paid back to you in spades.

If it is a Kiltie you appreciate, it may be paid back in scotch and haggis.

(If you are lucky the bottle of scotch will still be full!)

ଓଃୟୠ

Kiltology #409 - The Truth about Toys

I have learned one truth about toys and children.

It doesn't matter how many toys you buy or how amazing they are. If you have two kids in the same room they will invariably get into a fight over the same toy.

The power of the kilt has no affect on this issue. It can't do anything at all.

Kiltology #410 - Boots

It is utterly amazing the effect the proper pair of boots can have when complimenting a kilt.

They not only add additional height to the Kiltie, but an added measure of badassness.

Make sure when you make your kilt boot purchase that they not only fit your feet, but your entire personality.

That way they are the truest of complimentary accessories to the confidently kilted man.

Of course, they also make a great answer to the question.

ೞ ೲ

Kiltology #411 - Appearances
This is for the non-kilted haters out there.

Before you berate and ridicule the next Kiltie you happen upon due to his choice in clothing, keep these in mind:

~ He is not hiding his beliefs and ideals behind a socially normal garb and appearance.
~ He is not trying to be something he is not.
~ He is not putting forth a prim and proper public face when he is a menace to political correctness in private.
...
~ He is not not afraid to let people see who he really is.
~ He IS wearing and doing what he wants because he wants to, not because someone told him this is how he has to be.
~ He does not need to hide behind a dozen friends to speak his mind.
~ He is most likely far kinder, gentler and more trustworthy and loyal friend than you will ever be.

Kiltology #412 - Beliefs

Never, for a moment, assume that because a kitlie is standing next to you he believes any of the same things you do, or believes them the same way you do.

Assuming such and acting as such can have dire consequences, especially when you realize you have been talking to someone about something in which he has no interest at all. He is actually trying to get the attention of the bonnie lass behind you, but you just figured he was intently listening to you prattle on because he was facing you.

Ask first, then discuss. It will save you from embarrassing yourself publicly.

СВ∞

Kiltology #413 - Money

Learn to account for and budget your money early in life. This way you can enjoy all sorts of wonderful kilts and kit as you save more money

If you don't, I don't think debtor's prison is used anymore, you just get sued by your debt holders, lose all your stuff, and wind up begging mom to move back in with nothing.

Don't move back in with mom. Learn to manage your money.

Kiltology #414 - Mess

It is a relatively well know fact that a Kiltie being messy, yet organized, is commonplace.

The trouble is, when someone reorganizes the mess, it is impossible to find anything!

Moral of the story: DON'T MESS WITH A KILTIE'S MESS!!!

CB ED

Kiltology #415 - Cleaning

By definition, cleaning is simply shifting objects from one location to another.

So, knowing that we are just moving stuff around, if anyone has any kilts they need to clean, they can shift them to my location.

(FYI, NEVER clean a Kiltie's stuff without his prior approval and full acknowledgement. The results of doing so without his knowledge would be bad, to say the least!)

Kiltology #416 - A Kiltie's Daughter

If you find yourself where you fancy a Kiltie's daughter, know this:

You might as well just wait until the Kiltie is dead and gone before trying to court his daughter. The hell he will unleash upon you should you wrong his little princess is in every way far worse than anything in any holy book or horror movie out there.

He will be your father-in-law and he can most definitely go medieval on your ass.

CՑ ՑO

Kiltology #417 - How to Cause an Internet Panic

Here is a surefire way to cause a social media panic:

1. Take a picture of yourself wearing a kilt doing nothing special.
2. Post the picture on any of the major social networking sites.
3. Make sure at least one female has seen the picture.
4. Let simmer.

For added effect, add a second "action" pose photo. It is sure to cause all sorts of hell.

Kiltology #418 - Webcams

It is a little known fact that the invention of the webcam was actually commissioned by a group of kilt-loving lasses.

They had approached the inventor with a proposition. He created a camera small enough to be used on a computer that is able to broadcast anywhere in the world and he keeps all the credit and riches it would bring him.

The lasses only wanted a secret passcode so they could turn on the webcams in the bedrooms of slumbering Kilties to get a peek of the Kiltie and his kilt as it laid on the chair across the room.

(Now you know why there is a webcam on just about every laptop made!)

CS SO

Kiltology #419 - How to Get Rich

Here is the Kiltie's Guide to Getting Rich:

1. Obtain and wear kilt regularly.
2. Create and maintain relationships with all the new people you meet as a result of wearing the kilt.
3. Enjoy all the new opportunities presented to you as a result of wearing your kilt.
4. Go have fun with all the new people you met as a result of wearing your kilt.
5. If you are able, see #1 and repeat.

Kiltology #420 - Magic

There is one facet of magic you will seldom see on stage, advertised in a newspaper or promoted on the television.

This is the seemingly magical affect a kilt has on those surrounding its wearer.

~ The man wearing it is instantly more handsome.
~ Lasses flock to the kilt wearer for no other reason.
~ The wearer reaps the benefits of gifts and adoration those around him.
~ The kilt itself is seemingly indestructible, able to endure that which would destroy most every pair of p@nt$ out there.

There are many other magical benefits, these are just a few of the highlights.

છ૮૦

Kiltology #421 - Rides

Anything worth riding has handles.

Kiltology #422 - Eternity

Eternity is unique in that is has at least three very specific definitions to a Kiltie.

The first and most oft used definition is "Eternity is the time between when you pay for kilt and when it is delivered to your hands, sewn as ordered."

The popular term "jonseing" is in reference to the feeling a Kiltie feels while waiting the eternity between ordering and recieving a kilt.

The second, and more usable, yet less heard is, "eternity is the time between when I push the brew button on the coffee pot, and when it is ready to drink."

It is far less heard because anyone using this definition in the presence of a Kiltie is either extremely brave or married to the Kiltie, in which case you probably forced him out of bed to make you coffee anyway.

The third, which is one that enrages a great many Kiltie, is the time between when he gently reminds a group of teenagers that his "skirt" is a kilt and the time they finally bugger off to go make someone else's life miserable.

‮ଓ‭ ‮ଓ‭

Kiltology #423 - Proofing

Proofing your own book is easily one of the most infuriating processes known to man or pretty much any other intelligent species there is.

It is also the fastest way to tell yourself you are an idiot who is unable to use your native tongue properly.

ೞ೩ ೱ೦

Kiltology #424 - Waiting

Waiting Sucks.

Anyone who tells you differently has never had to wait for anything, thereby surrendering in the battle of wits before it has even begin.

Kiltology #425 - Most Difficult Time

The most difficult time to deal with children is NOT
Christmas morning, at a ceremony, a library, or any other
place where they are supposed to behave.

It is when they have both finished their waffles and the suger
rush kicks in from the syrup ... and your coffee has NOT
kicked in.

CB ED

Kiltology #426 - Pomp and Celebration

While a great many successful people revel in the massive,
public celebrations of their success, the Kiltie is busy doing
equally great things behind the scenes, making huge efforts to
succeed without all the partying and back-patting.

Don't get me wrong, Kilties LOVE a good party. We just
don't need a parade and party in our honor because we did
the right thing.

Kiltology #427 - Can't

Be warned. Telling a Kiltie he can't do something is like trying to tell a 2-year-old she can't play with her new dollhouse on Christmas morning after she just tore through ALL her christmas candy.

You will regret it and then most likely have to clean up after the Kiltie has finished doing whatever you said he couldn't do.

☙❦❧

Kiltology #428 - Time

Time is of the utmost importance to a Kiltie, and has very peculiar actions when in the proximity of said Kiltie.

~ When walking through unknown territory, time definitly slows to a standstill.
~ When talking to a bonnie lass, it goes all sorts of haywire.
~ When having a pint with friends, it seems to speed up to the point you completely lose track of it.
~ When you are in trouble with the missus, it leaves you high and dry to deal with her on your own.

Kiltology #429 - Worth

The worth of a man should not be measured by his material posessions or potential ability to help.

The worth of a man is measured by the use of his capacity to help others who cannot help themselves without regard of recompense.

Even a man of boundless riches in gold and land can be considered worthless if he does not help those truly in need.

*This has no bearing on the lazy masses who have the capacity to help themselves and choose not to. Those who sit around complaining about how hard life is without lifting a finger to improve their situation do not need help. They need to grow up and accept responsibility for the results of their lack of action.

CB ED

Kiltology #430 - Awesome

The determination of how awesome a Kiltie is CANNOT be measured by what everyone knows he has done.

It is measured by the things he does without anyone knowing, just because the are the right things to do.

This makes it very hard to know who is awesome, as the most awesome people spend their time doing, not gloating about the one thing they did.

To find an awesome Kiltie, talk to his friends instead. They will know.

Kiltology #431 - Plumber's Crack

It is a little known fact that p@nt$ that ride too low were made the default uniform for plumbers by husbands in Scotland.

They found their kilt-loving wives would stay home and watch the kilted plumber fixing the pipes under sink. Then the lass would break or clog the kitchen sink on purpose so the kilted plumber would have to come back often to check their pipes again.

The low-riding p@nt$ were enforced as they are FAR less enticing to the ladies.

(If you have no idea what I'm talking about, just imagine a guy in a kilt working on the pipes under the kitchen sink ... ladies try not to giggle or blush.)

∽◌◌◌◌∽

Kiltology #432 - Subtlety

The art of subtlety was perfected early in kilted history.

When a Kiltie wanted to gain the attention of a bonnie lass, he would nonchalantly meander toward her, kilt fitted just perfectly, and try to throw a caber over her head.

The Kilties who managed to impress a lass and escort her home were the ones who didn't kill the poor lass by dropping a tree on her.

Kiltology #433 - Natural Selection

Contrary to popular belief, Darwin did NOT devise his theory of Natural Selection over years of observation, study, and research into the habits of species around the world.

He concluded his entire body of work in the span of a single weekend in a small kilted community, whilst having a few meals at the local pub. His conclusions were reached as he watched men wearing p@nt$ vainly attempt to attract the shapely lasses and determined that the evolution of the kilted male led to his unwavering victory in his selection of lasses for procreation and continuation of the species.

He also determined that the evolution of single malt ran concurrently with the kilt, as the more Kilties who arrived, the more wildly varied the selection of single malt became!

CB&O

Kiltology #434 - Philosophy

The commonly accepted evolution of Philosphical Thought is pretty well documented.

The biggest questions are generally accepted to be:

"Why?"

"Who am I?"

"Why am I here?"

and

"Where is my towel?"

What is NOT documented is the very first question in the history of histories, which is:

"What is up his kilt?"

☙ ❧

Kiltology #435 - Revolution

It is well known that the Earth spins around, giving us night and day.

What is not well known is why.

In the earliest of times, when the kilt was first worn, there was no day and night. The Earth went 'round the sun, but did not spin on its own.

The Mother of the Universe, seeing the glory of the kilt, was trying to get a peek up the kilt. The Kiltie was walking away, so she set the world a turning so he would not leave her view.

As you can probably guess, she never did get to see what she was looking for, as the Earth is spinning to this day.

CRANCES

Kiltology #436 - Politics

For the Kilted world, politics are easy.

If you can't solve a problem over a few pints or wee drams ... everyone finds a big tree and throws them at each other.

Last one standing wins.

(How you fall is irrelevant. Not handling your whisky is grounds for a loss in most any political arena.)

Kiltology #437 - Lamp Shades

Have you ever noticed that many lamp shades seem to have the same basic shape as a kilt?

Wanna know why?

The lass who invented the lamp shade were so enamored by the kilt and all the glory held beneath it, she created a covering for the lamp in the kilt's shape. The lamp's warming glow cascading over them from beneath the 'kilt', putting a warm red glow on all their cheeks as most lamp shades sit atop a single supporting tower.

(I'll bet none of the lasses reading this will look at a lamp shade the same again!)

⟨ॐ ॐ⟩

Kiltology #438 - Satisfaction

Satisfaction is something women with men in p@nt$ complain about all the time ...

... and women with Kilties keep to themselves!

Kiltology #439 - Time Management

If you ever happen upon a Kiltie just sitting on his ass, enjoying a pint in the evening, don't give him any crap about being lazy, worthless, or a drain on the community.

Odds are he did more by nine am today than you did all week. He just needs a pint and few hours of rest before getting back to it.

Oh, and he will most likely be none too receptive of your comment and will retort with a wit as sharp as a knife.

CB SO

Kiltology #440 – Genius

Genius starts really small.

First, it could be a creative way to find a pint.

It could then progress to a means by which said pint can be obtained without actually leaving the chair.

It grows into a more serious level of brilliance when the beverage is not only proper temperature, but is in a proper container, which you didn't have when the process started.

True genius, of course is simply showing up and the pint appears from nowhere.

(Then again, this happens to most every Kiltie I've ever met the moment we enter the pub, so you there you go.)

Kiltology #441 - Yo Momma

I was in a pub once, hearing some folks joking around. This is what I heard:

Guy in kilt: (laughing after a joke)
Guy in p@nt$: Oh yeah? Yo momma...

THWACK THUD CRASH

Guy in p@nt$: What the hell are you doing (as he tries to pick himself up off the floor)?

Guy in kilt: Don't you dare insult my mother.

(Guy in p@nt$ picks himself up from across the bar, and his friends escort him to the hospital to remove the barstool from his head.)

Morale of the story: Don't mess with a Kiltie's mom!

CB&O

Kiltology #442 - Reality

Reality is that moment when you realize the pot of gold at the end the rainbow, the one you have spent countless years chasing instead of spending time with your friends and family, only contains that which you brought with you.

And in many cases, after years of searching, all that can be put in the pot is a lifetime of dreams put aside in favor of the search of riches.

A gentle word. Keep looking for that pot of gold, but be sure you bring enough with you to fill it with a lifetime of wondrous experiences with amazing friends and family.

Oh, and make sure you bring a wee green kilt. I'm pretty sure the leprechaun's p@nt$ are in dire need of a wash.

CB ED

Kiltology #443 - Permission

Consider it the start of an amazing day when your 3-year-old daughter not only gives you permission to make coffee BEFORE tending to her 5,380 immediate needs, but also indicates which kilt she will allow those around her to wear in her presence.

Today is going to be a good day.

(She picked my green Utilikilt AND Wyvern Sporran. I still have some work to do with her on what accessories goes with what types of kilt.)

Kiltology #444 - Sarcasm

Sarcasm :

~ A viable, self-sustaining, eloquent form of communication far more advanced than any common language.
~ Not to be uses casually or without regard for the consequences.
~ Has more variance and subtlety than all the languages of the world combined.
~ Can be the most evil in meaning while sounding like sirens in the moonlight.
~ Must be left to the professionals. Rookies will just get hurt.
~ Genetically found in a vast majority of Kilties. Be assured they are far more sarcastic than anyone in p@nt$ and wield that sarcasm with expertise and finesse that would make Michelangelo jealous.

☙❧

Kiltology #445 - Initiative

While you sit and grumble over how something is supposed to be done, who is going to approve it, and who is going to take the blame if it fails, odds are a Kiltie has already taken it upon himself to just get it done without all the BS.

In all reality, he probably finished whatever you were debating before you even finished talking about it!

Kiltology #446 - A Perfect Moment

The definition of a perfect moment varies wildly from person to person, more so among Kilties.

This moment I'm quite certain will fit most everyone definition of a perfect moment.

This morning, while getting the kids ready for the day, I sat on the couch for a moment in a vain attempt to wake up.

Both my wonderful children decided it was an opportune time to dog pile and tickle daddy with insane yet joyous cackles filling the air.

They proceeded to attempt to tickle for a few moments until I retaliated, getting them both laughing hysterically.

I stopped tickling them a few seconds later and they both just laid there, quietly holding me and each other.

I know it was only a minute or so, but for those scant few moments the entire world could have stopped and it would have been fine. We were happy.

That was a perfect moment I will not ever forget.

CB ED

Kiltology #447 - Happiness

Want to get happy? here is a simple guide.

1. Buy kilt (any kilt will do so long as it fits).

2. Remove p@nt$ (assistance preferred but not necessary).

3. Put on kilt (again, assistance preferred but not necessary).

4. Crumple p@nt$ in a worthless pile on a non-flamable surface with plenty of open air.

5. Light match.

6. Put match on p@nt$. Make sure there are no flammable materials around, and you are not currently under a burn ban.

7. Dance around like a child with a new toy as you revel in your newly found freedom and happiness as the p@nt$ transition from a painful man-trap to a pile of smoldering ash being returned to the Earth from whence they came.

8. If your assistant is still around and giving you 'that look', thank your assistant in the best way you know that won't get you slapped too hard.

9. Thank assistant again if you can.

Kiltology #448 - Filter

I've heard a great many times that Kilties have no 'filter' from folks who (obviously) are not kilted.

I strongly disagree.

Were a Kiltie to need a filter, he can simply pour the beverage which needs to be filtered either through his kilt or into his gullet.

Either way, whatever it was that needed to be filtered will come out filtered in some manner.

Odds are the beverage will NOT go through the kilt, as it is not fresh from the wash and the Kiltie won't want to risk staining the kilt. It is best to let him filter it the old fashioned way, just don't expect to get any of the beverage back in a drinkable form.

CB❧

Kiltology #449 – Observation

Kilties out there, pay very close attention to those around you, especially the lasses.

Learn to read their body language, signals and understand what they are trying to say without speaking.

For those who are extremely skilled, you can determine everything that could be said in a discussion well before any words are exchanged.

(Especially if her hands are warm!)

Kiltology #450 - Balls

Balls are found EVERYWHERE in life!

~ They bounce around from here to there when in motion.

~ They sit still when not going anywhere.

~ They seem to have a natural attraction and
curiosity about them.

~ They are almost always the topic of conversation when
they are around a kilt.

~ Stepping on them can cause a great amount of pain.

~ They make a clanging sound when bouncing together.

~ Many fear them falling on their head.

~ They are guarded fiercely by their owners.

~ The bigger they are, the more proud their owner is.

~ They can mesmerize when when rolled around
in one's hand.

~ They are seldom receptive to anything cold.

~ They are best left to be handled by someone skilled in their
use.

෩෨

Kiltology #451 - Seasonal Allergies

It is a little known fact that seasonal allergies are not just a random medical condition, but a concerted act of biological warfare against Kilties by none other than Mother Nature herself.

When She realized men would no longer bend to her will after they had donned The Kilt and found their new freedom, Mother Nature released into the atmosphere an evil biological attack on Kilties in the form of mold, pollen, and all manner of airborne microbes designed to make the Kiltie as miserable as possible. While it is a nuisance to some, and a huge pain to others, this feeble attempt to keep us Kilties down has failed with the advent of a myriad of anti-allergy medicines and treatments.

Again, Mother Nature doesn't get her wish and will undoubtedly come up with some other devious means of ending Kiltie freedom (or at least getting a glimpse of their kilted pride!)

CB ED

Kiltology #452 – Affection

As is well known, there are more ways to show your affection to another than hairs on most of our heads.

That being said, if you feel affection for another, be sure to SHOW that affection through your actions and deeds.

The most heartfelt affection shown only through words is just another story being told, with nothing to back up those words besides hot air.

And without actions behind those words, the target of your verbal affection will most likely find someone else, who knows how to do more than simply speak.

☙❧

Kiltology #453 - Support

Support has a great deal of varied meanings.

The most important meaning of support is that structure of friends, family, and acquaintances a Kiltie has to successfully meet his personal, psychological, and social needs. Without this support most any Kiltie will simply go mad, and maybe even start wearing p@nt$!

The second most important meaning of proper support prevents a woman's boobs from moving in with her belly button.

Which of the above is actually most important varies from Kiltie to Kiltie.

Kiltology #454 - Arguing

If you want to be sure you are in for a very lengthy, drawn out discourse on any topic you chose, make a point opposite a Kiltie's and stick to it.

You will almost certainly remain arguing with the Kiltie, who will also refuse to give his ground, until well after any sane folks would have simply given up and gone home.

In extreme cases, you may be handed the keys to the establishment and instructed to close down when you finish if the owner has been through this before.

෫෨෫෮

Kiltology #455 – Introspection

sit quietly

you and your thoughts

nothing else
no talking
no playing
no working
no outside influences

just you and your thoughts

now think about those things for which you have no
explanation

think long and hard
do not seek an answer

just think

be at peace with yourself
and everything around you

be calm

be still

know yourself

understand yourself

be at peace with yourself.

Kiltology #456 - Gentle Folk

For the most part, with our crazy stories, crazier habits and die-hard individuality, we Kilties are generally a gentle folk once you get to know us.

Hard working, self-reliant, and loyal to a fault.

Be sure you don't cross a Kiltie, especially with regards to his friends and family.

There be dragons there. Dragons you and your kid's kids won't soon forget.

CR&

Kiltology #457 - Concrete

Concrete. Rock Solid Concrete.

That is what your sinus cavity feels like when you are actually allergic to an entire state.

The kilt has no power to prevent this unless you wear it on your head, which we all know is not a good idea if you are the one originally wearing it on your waist.

Besides, having a kilt on your head brings consequences of its own.

Kiltology #458 - Persistance

For the average Kiltie, persistence is a built-in quality.

What does that mean?

If a Kiltie gets something stuck in his head, he will move
Heaven and Earth to make it a reality.

So, word to the wise: Never get between a Kiltie and his
goals. It could end badly for you.

CB ᘓᗌ

Kiltology #459 - Speed

Speed is extremely important to many a Kiltie.

The speed at which a Kiltie can remove his kilt and kit in low
light may have a very serious impact on his ability to progress
from speaking to a bonnie lass to something more.

Kiltology #460 - Kilted Fitness and the Female Response

It is a well documented fact that the average female responds to a fit, athletic looking man far better than one who has spent the past 10 years on the couch.

Lucky for us Kilties, the act of simply donning the kilt removes at least 5 of those years, giving us an advantage when it comes to going from couch-man to lady-killer.

Also, once we do get those last 5 years worked off, even the most Adonis-like male in p@nt$ is put to shame by a man in a kilt.

Moral of the story: Kilt up often and always. Chicks dig it.

CRWSO

Kiltology #461 - Corners

I've discovered a couple more things that all the mystical abilities of the kilt are powerless against:

Cabinet corners, doors, and freezer doors.

If I mash my skull into another corner of the cabinet or its door again, I swear there will be an impromptu remodel with a large sledge and chainsaw.

Yes, I have a mean headache and another dent in my head. Not happy about this at all.

Kiltology #462 - Kilts and Chocolate

What do kilts and chocolate have in common?

Women should enjoy them both, equally and often.

ಚಿ৪೦

Kiltology #463 - Beer

It is a common misconception that beer was invented as a nutritional supplement as normal foodstuffs would spoil much faster than a stout beer.

The truth is far less noble.

Beer was in fact invented by the p@nt$-wearing gents of old. They had LOADS of time on their hands and needed something to drown their sorrows, as all the lasses were off with the kilt-like garment wearing gents ensuring the continuation of the species.

Whisky, on the other hand, was invented as a cure-all by the kilted folks of old. Beer just wasn't doing the job and gents in p@nt$ couldn't stomach the power of aqua vitae.

Kiltology #464 - Fashion

It is a well known fact that Kilties are at the forefront of the fashion world.

Everyone who is anyone has been seen in a kilt and it shall continue to be this way for all time.

The best part is, no matter what is done to make the kilt different, special or unique...

...it will always be a kilt.

ೞ೩ఙ

Kiltology #465 - Hernia

While it is overwhelmingly well known among Kilties how the dreaded hernia check is performed, it is not at all well known how such an invasive and uncomfortable procedure came into being.

The first checks were not performed by doctors trying to further the advance of medicine, but by bonnie lasses looking for an excuse to get under man's kilt. It was only after enough lasses who happened to be nurses found that those who appeared injured from prolonged and vigorous battle tended to react differently to the aforementioned checks that a doctor investigated further and discovered the hernia.

From this point on it became a medical procedure generally perfomed by male doctors, taking all the fun out of it for those of us who aren't injured.

For any lasses reading, this does NOT mean you should relegate the all-important kilt check to doctors. You need your fun too!

CB EO

Kiltology #466 - Voting

When dealing with Kilties do not, for the love of all that is holy, think you have the all-powerful ability to sway his judgement or change his ideals and way of thinking, especially during an election.

Trying to change how a Kiltie thinks, or votes in this case, is like trying to do a frame-up restore of a 1964 ½ Mustang Convertible with only a broken wooden spoon as your tool kit.

If you don't believe me, just ask a Kiltie's wife. There is a reason Scottish wives invented the rolling pin, and it had nothing to do with making bread.

⊂ঃ৪০

Kiltology #467 - Rolling Pins

Most folks in the world know a rolling pin is used to flatten dough for baking.

What few know of its true origin.

The rolling pin was initially invented by the wives of Kilties as a means to change their minds. A small caber was first used, but was found to be cumbersome and unwieldy. The caber was cut down with a handle carved in the end. It only took a few weeks before one of these was found in most every home in the land, especially those close to pubs.

Only after one of these lasses got angry at some pie dough she was working with and clubbed it did she realize this 'husband tamer' had other less destructive, more productive uses.

The rolling pin, as it was now called, was immediately welcome in homes across the world, with its nefarious true use secreted away to the inner circles on women everywhere.

Kilties, be sure to check your house for one of these things and hide it.

☙❧

Kiltology #468 – Conflict

Within every Kiltie, there are two men fighting for who will be the one in charge, constantly in constant with each other.

The first is what everyone sees, the confident kilt-wearing man. With a certain allure, mystery, and strength about him. People ask him questions becuase he looks like he knows the answer, no matter what the question is. Lasses want to know him, both personally and biblically. Men want to be him, to know the freedom and joy that is wearing a kilt. He tends to exude confidence and the ability to handle pretty much everything. He has an obvious and fierce loyalty to his family and bretheren and a Santa Clause-like joviality and zest for life. This is one of the men living within him.

The other man is the side that is not easily seen and less often shown publically. It is the teddy bear that lives within the Kiltie. His close friends and famly know he is a pushover when his children or other children give him 'that look' and start giggling. Puppy kisses and babies make him smile on the inside. He is tender and caring, but this side is usually very far from the surface and at odds with his other self at all times. This is the other man living within the Kiltie.

Some Kilties handle this conflict with ease and venture between each as the time arises, others drift towards one side or the other depending on his personality, experience, and circumstances.

Regardless of which side of the spectrum the Kiltie may live on, rest assured he is the one person you want on your side, especially when there is fun to be had or trouble that needs tending to.

Kiltology #469 - Gross

It is well known the traditional Kiltie wears only what he was born with 'neath his kilt.

In my travels amongst the non-kilted, I've heard many folks say it is 'gross' to not wear underwear.

For those who think it is gross, do me a quick favor. Look at the coffee mug you take in the car.

I'm certain you drank from it this morning while it was in dire need of a trip to the seldom-seen kitchen sink for a deep cleaning.

Here is the really gross part. You put your mouth on that filthy thing EVERY morning.

Next time you think a Kiltie's dress habits are gross, take a look at your morning coffee routine first before passing judgement.

ᏣᏃ

Kiltology #470 - Discovery

The journey of self discovery is filled with introspection, reflection, and a humbling moment when you realize how you fit into your particular version of the world.

It is then filled with copious amounts of fellowship and imbibing as you share your new found enlightenment with all your friends.

You then spend the rest of the evening spouting drunken philosophical ramblings to anyone who will listen.

You wake up the next morning, trying to figure out what in hell happened and where your kilt has gone walkabout to.

And then the trip begins as you try to discover yourself, the reason for your excruciating headache, and where the bottle of aspirin is.

CB ED

Kiltology #471 - Nothing

Nothing is a VERY meaningful word in the kilted universe.

~ Nothing is what is worn under a kilt. It all works just fine!
~ Nothing is left after Kilties conquer a foreign land.
~ Nothing is what you find in the pub after a
kilted pub crawl.
~ Nothing is what you get from a Kiltie if you don't ask for it
in plain english (or whatever their native tongue is).
~ Nothing is the contents of a Kiltie's pantry after having
friends over 'for a nightcap'.

Similarly,

~ None is the amount of BS a Kiltie will put up with if you
mess with his friends and family.
~ Nowhere is where you will get for making fun of or
insulting a Kiltie for his choice of clothing.
~ No one will convince me that wearing a kilt is wrong, evil,
or will otherwise make me less of a man.

Lastly,

~ Never is how often you will catch me in a shower wearing
a kilt.

☙❧

Kiltology #472 - Single

For the kilted man, the word 'single' can have two vastly different meanings depending on his situation.

For the single Kiltie with a decent job and no kids, it means the party is on. He has the ability to venture out in the world and cause as much 'trouble' as he sees fit or that his friends will let him get away with. He becomes the life of the party and is loads of fun to hang around with.

For the single Kiltie WITH children, it is a turning point in his life. In most cases, he grows an even bigger pair, takes full responsibility for his kids, and works his ass off to give them the very best childhood he can with what he has. He sacrifices his own personal wants and needs to ensure that his kids are well taken care of and provided for. He goes to the ends of the Earth to ensure no harm befalls his children. Or, he bails on his kids completely and becomes a black mark on Kilties everywhere; an oxygen thief robbing good people of good air.

Personally, I think any Kiltie who bails on their kids like that is unfit to wear the kilt and deserves the torture that is wearing p@nt$ every day for the rest of his life.

CBEO

Kiltology #473 - Santa and Scotch

It is widely known that children around the world leave snacks and drink for Santa on Christmas eve. The snacks vary from country to country; here in the US milk and cookies are the norm.

On the very first Christmas, the kilted folks left a dram of scotch and a wee roll for Santa. It was regarded as the greatest Christmas of all time by the children of Kilties, as they received massive amounts of gifts, especially those further down the delivery list.

The day after Christmas, on the other hand, was regarded as the worst peacetime day in kilted history. Santa had come home to Mrs. Claus so drunk that he tried to get VERY frisky with her, passed out, woke up, walked out into the toy factory without his p@nt$, and passed out again in a pile of chocolate candies, half of them eaten, the other half melted and matted in his beard. The elves drew all over him in markers. Mrs. Claus was not impressed.

Mrs. Claus made a trip to every single kilted house the following night and walloped every Kiltie over the head with a club VERY hard. She assured them she would return if it ever happened again, with a club for the Kiltie and a bigger club for the scotch cabinet. She also said the elves would stop making scotch for good Kilties everywhere.

Scotch was never again left out for Santa. He was not happy and started handing out coal for bad kids the next year.

CB80

Kiltology #474 - Santa and Coal

It is well known that bad children get coal in their stockings from Santa.

It is NOT well known as to why coal was chosen from all the undesirable things a child could get, or even nothing at all.

The truth is that Santa really enjoys a wee nip o' the water of life, and the smell of coal almost perfectly masks the smell of a good peaty single malt.

CB❦SO

Kiltology #475 - Santa's Helpers

As is quite well known, Santa's helpers consist of an army of male elves who can do damn near everything.

What it NOT well known is that years ago, Santa had both male and female helpers.

No, Mrs. Claus did not evict them. She actually enjoyed the banter with them as they worked on Christmas toys. The lasses themselves chose to leave. On one Christmas eve a female helper accompanied Santa on his rounds and one stop in Scotland changed the history of Christmas.

Santa and his helper ventured into the house, which was obviously the host of a Christmas celebration earlier, as there were decorations everywhere and the cookie tray and punch bowl were on the kitchen counter, empty.

The helper was putting a present under the tree, and turned to notice the male occupant of the house asleep on the couch. He was still wearing his kilt, but it was askew with his kilted pride in plain view of the now intrigued elfin lass. She repositioned the kilt and left a wee blue ribbon for the lucky Kiltie.

When she returned home, she shared this story with the rest of the lasses, her face glowing like she was opening her own Christmas presents. They promptly submitted their resignations and all ventured out to seek more Kilties.

They never returned, much to the chagrin of the male elves.

Kiltology #476 - Crow

Crow is a staple in the diet of some Kilties.

Especially when he thinks he has had an epiphany and is reminded by all his friends and family that he sounds like his p@nt$ are on too tight.

C33 80

Kiltology #477 - Resolutions

The New Year's Resolution is a promise made every year, a goal you set to accomplish for yourself.
The very first New Year's Resolution was actually a Hogmanay Resolution. It was a bonnie lass, saying "I will see what is under that lad's kilt before this night is through!"
There is no evidence of her success or failure, but I don't know a single bonnie Scottish lass who doesn't get what she wants!

Kiltology #478 - Neverending

There are few things on this Earth that are neverending:

~ The number of questions a child will ask between waking
up and going to sleep, every day.
~ The time it seems to take between ordering and receiving a
kilt, especially a custom one!
~ The amount of agony endured by wearing garments with
individual leg holes.

and, without a doubt...

~ The number of times a lass will try to kilt check a Kiltie
regardless of how many times she has checked him
previously.

CB ED

Kiltology #479 - Change And Choice

As a Kiltie, change is an accepted fact of life. Most of us
made the choice to change our clothing, which, in turn, is
followed by a change in lifestyle. There are many aspects of
being kilted which are not normally found among the non-
kilted, like sporran management and pleat checking. In
making the choice to change, embracing the kilt, we also
change our social status. We unintentionally become a font
of knowledge, being asked every manner of question. This
choice to wear the kilt puts us squarely in the limelight no
matter where we are. Choosing to wear the kilt is a major and
bold change. Do not tread this lightly, but when you do,
enjoy all the benefits you will reap from joining the ranks of
the kilted.

Kiltology #480 - Diamonds

It is a fairly well known fact that diamonds are a girl's best
friend. What is not well known is why. Sure, they are sparkly
and rare, but the true story is this:
A diamond with all its rare sparkle and expense is FAR easier
to find than a strapping lad in a kilt. A man in a kilt is always
a far better friend than a shiny rock on your finger, especially
when Mother Nature whips his kilt around for the lasses.
How many diamonds have you seen roof a house, fix the car,
clear the plumbing, AND cook a mean boxty all while
wearing a well-placed kilt!

CR80

Kiltology #481 - Ya Know?

Ya Know?

When ya know, ya know.

If ya don't know, then you need to know, ya know?

So know what ya know, and then get to knowin' what ya
don't know,
ya know?

Kiltology #482 - Leather Kilt

It is well known that the kilt has an almost aphrodisiac-like quality to it. It attracts anyone who likes the kilt. A kilt made of leather or pseudo-leather is a completely different animal for many people. Wearing this kind of kilt is like marching a fresh steak into a den of famished hyenas, and you are the steak. This counts doubly so if you are the only single guy around.

Consider yourself warned.

ℭ℘℘

Kiltology #483 - A Man In A Kilt

A man in a kilt
Sliding down the brass firepole
Women everywhere swoon

Kiltology #484 - Wind

Wind Blows
Kilt sways
Blush

ೞ ೲ

Kiltology #485 - Ahead

Ahead is a mythical place where most people are trying to get,
but none ever get there and stay for very long. In this mytical
place, the house is always clean, dishes and laundry are done,
bills are paid, and you are perpetually happy. This place does
exist, but can only be visited for VERY short periods of time.
In reality, there will always be another mess to clean, there
will always be dishes and clothes to wash, there will always be
bills, and you will not always be happy.
The only time all this goes away is when you are six feet
under, and you can't share your kilt with a world from a box
in the ground.
So, stop trying to stay ahead all the time, kilt up and enjoy the
life you have. Go do something fun with friends and family,
even if just a walk in the park. Live for life, not for the
dishwasher or bill collector.

Kiltology #486 - Go

Go

Put on your kilt

Venture into the p@nt$ world

Hold your head up high

Go

ᬀ᭙

Kiltology #487 - Jokes

If you can tell all your good kilted jokes in front of children,
you don't know any good kilted jokes.

Kiltology #488 - Lackadaisical

The word lackadaisical does not mean he who is lacking daisies. It is the representation of a general malaise among many folks who expect a miracle, or someone to handle their responsibilities without any effort on their part. For some who are honestly working hard to make it work, the effort isn't enough. Those who simply don't try and expect the same or better results are lackadaisical.

How does this apply to the Kilt?

The act of simply wearing a kilt the first time takes a great deal of effort and determination. Nothing lackadaisical there.

ငဒ ၉ဂ

Kiltology #489 - Doesn't Like the Kilt

If someone tells you they don't like your kilt tell them this: "Would you rather I take it off now?"

(This also works as a fun line with the lasses.)

EXECUTE AT YOUR OWN RISK!
By taking this advice, you agree any results of your actions are your own responsibility and will not come after me for bail, hospital bills, or helping to find your kilt the next morning.

Kiltology #490 - Unaware

The oddest throught I've had lately is that if you stood an average guy in a decently-made kilt, average non-factory-made sporran, boots,and t-shirt with a bunch of guys in tailored three-piece suits, the guy in the kilt will NEVER be picked as the one with the most expensive wardrobe. Just something I thought of as I considered what I put on to go to wal-mart compared to the office and found my work clothes are FAR cheaper.

$$\text{CS 8O}$$

Kiltology #491 - Fire Alarms

When at the pub, be very leery of anyone who tells you to leave your beverage on the bar if the fire alarm goes off, especially if they are not kilted. Many a times has the alarm gone off and all the beers on the bar wind up empty. UNWISE is he who drains a Kiltie's drink whilst he is not at the bar.

Even more unwise is the Kiltie who leaves his beverage untended to, but that is another story altogether.

Kiltology #492 - Cougars

Recent discoveries have determined that Kilties do in fact have a natural predator:

The Cougar.

Cougars tend to roam in pairs or small packs and can be found in most pubs and taverns across the kilted universe. They seem benign at first, but as they consume alcoholic beverages, their true nature becomes evident. They will do damn near anything to get under a Kiltie's kilt, regardless of local ordinances, laws, or even common decency.

BE WARNED!

The Cougar is a VERY difficult predator to evade and even worse once told (rather loudly and bluntly, mind you) that all her efforts are in vain, and that you would rather wear p@nt$ than continue any further discussions or activities with her.

It has very recently been observed that there are Cougars in the wild whom any Kiltie would be VERY happy to be stalked by, so this no longer applies to ALL Cougars. Be sure to keep your wits about you, gents.

CB ED

Kiltology #493 - Hugs

Common knowledge tells us the average Kiltie is a man and a half, can do most anything without training, and is able to make even the most miserable of times a hell of a party. It is less commonly known that the hugs from his children will melt his gruff, stoic exterior to reveal the teddy bear within, full of joy, happiness, and love.

Don't tell any Kilties I told you this.

They will most certainly remind me exactly how gruff they can be!

CB ED

Kiltology #495 - Happiness

The happiest moment of this Kiltie's life is every moment I spend with my kids, seeing the joy and awe on their faces as they finally get to experience all the things I used to do as a child in my hometown. It is easily the most amazing feeling to see their eyes wide with wonder every day something new is discovered and experienced.

Yes, this is true happiness.

Kiltology #494 - Kilt Ninjas At It Again

If you see them let me know. I know they exist, just cant find them. I think they stole my leather kilt...it is gone again. :(

ॐ॰

Kiltology #496 - Sewing

If you happen upon a kilted lad who is sewing his damaged kilt, please let the poor lad to his work and be on your way. He is trying quite diligently to repair his clothes so he can avoid being taken off to the stocks for public nudity.

Kiltology #497 - Kilts At Work

When deciding on what kilt to wear to work (I sit in front of a computer for eons at a time). I have opted to wear a modern utility-style kilt almost exclusively. Here is why:

1. Far less fabric to manage when sitting for long periods of time.
2. Not as much of a heat trap.
3. Sewn-down pleats are far easier to manage.
4. It is FAR less expensive for a decent utility kilt as opposed to a good tartan kilt.
5. No sporran to deal with.
6. No massive buckle to mess with.
7. You can chuck it in the wash if you spill lunch on it.
8. Modesty snaps on some for when you swivel around rapidly.
9. FAR easier to repair if a seam pops.

ဤ ၈ဢ

Kiltology #498 - A Wise Man

I once asked a wise man how he became so wise.
He simply stated: "Nothing".

My head exploded right there.
(See #471)

Kiltology #499 - Wisdom

How wise is the wisest of the wise if that wisdom is kept to himself?

(No, that isn't a quote from anyone but myself as far as google can tell me.)

CB ∞

Kiltology #500 - Surfing

If you have not been surfing, go do it. Keep these few things in mind:

1. A kilt is a sail strapped to your waist. If it is windy, you will go where the wind pushes you.
2. A wetsuit or speedo is recommended. Surfing regimental will almost certainly give EVERYONE on the beach a show.
3. If you haven't been surfing before, you will be sore in places you have never thought you could be sore.
4. You will have one hell of a time even if you don't even stand up for one wave. It is an amazing experience.
5. Wear a LIGHT kilt. A modern kilt or traditional wool will weigh you down a LOT.
6. Did I mention it is awesome? You will have one hell of a good time!
7. If you can, find someone to get pics. Kilted surfing is great and needs to be enjoyed by all!

(If you do wear a speedo under the kilt, yellow with a smiley face is the preferred design.)

Kiltology #501 - Beer

Beer is your friend.
It may not be a daily companion,
or even someone you visit once in a blue moon.
It may even be someone you never speak to … ever.
But when the fit hits the shan,
a single glass of brew is there for you.

CЗ Яࠏ

Kiltology #502 - Freedom

Freedom in our kilted world is sought daily, not only from
uncomfortable bifurcated garments, but from that which
holds us back.
Freedom from oppression, tyranny, and evil.
Personal freedom to think, wonder, and grow as
we feel is right.
Freedom to explore both the world we live in and the world
in our own minds.
Most important in this search for freedom is the freedom to
be who we are and live as we do, without being forced to
exist as an automaton, grinding out the day in someone else's
image of how you are to be.

Live your own life

Be true to your self

Know yourself inside and out.

Kilt on!

Kiltology #503 - Volume

Yelling at a man in a kilt is not going to get you very good results. Yelling louder will get even worse results. Screaming and whining in a high, shrill voice will bring upon you the wrath of angry ancient Celtic Gods ... even if the man in the kilt isn't A Celt!

(If you are the 5-year-old-daughter of said man in a kilt, go scream in your room. He is trying to save the world.)

ଓଃ ଽ୦

Kiltology #504 - Courage

Courage is a wonderful thing. It is the ability to tell your fears and anxieties to go play in traffic while you lead an awesome life.
Courage is what you have when you strap on a kilt and wear it as you see fit, where you want, and ignore the comments and negativity that can sometime follow a man in a kilt.
Courage is being yourself, living your life the way you want to.

Courage is being kilted.

Kiltology #505 - Confidence

I am asked "how can you wear that everywhere?" fairly often by people who can't see themelves in a kilt. Like them, I was cautious in the beginning. I was worried about what people would say, how they would react, and how it would be received by friends and family. Somewhere in that early time I realized that it really doesn't matter what people think about the kilt. They can accept me for who I am or they can reject me. Folks who rejected me obviously were not really interested in me as a person, so no big loss. That knowledge gave me the confidence to wear it more often and eventually to incorporate it into my worklife as a way to stand out in a crowd of business suit-clad professionals. It is that confidence that I hope to instill in anyone reading this who is still on the fence about wearing a kilt outside of a parade or festival.

If you like the kilt for whatever reason, wear it.

ೞ౫౩

Kiltology #506 - Mother Nature

I have often wondered why it is windy outside almost every day I am kilted. I also wondered why it happens more when I spend some time putting together what I am wearing and not just throwing on the first kilt I find.

I realized why this morning.

A good strong wind is Mother Nature's way of saying "Nice Kilt".

Kiltology #507 - Bravado

Since my return to the snowy white north, I have been asked repeatedly why I am not kilted all the time. As most of the connected world knows, there has been record snowfall in New England totalling over 9 feet this winter. For those who don't wear the kilt, dragging one's bits and pieces around in really deep snow is not something I suggest.

Can you imagine this scenario playing out at the local emergency room?

You: "Ma'am, I think I have frostbite. Can you take a look at this?"

Bonnie nurse: "Your fingers, toes, and nose all look fine. Those are the places you normally get frostbite first. Why do you think you have frostbite?"

You: …

You: (lifting your sporran and kilt) "You didn't check everything."

The smart kilt wearer knows that bravado must give way to common sense in the blustery winter months to prevent the above senario.

CB ℰᴐ

KiltsRock.com

Kevin M. Thompson founded the Brotherhood of the Kilt in 2007, which quickly became a strong foundation for support, advice, confidence building, and story sharing for the Kilted Community. It would be through this avenue that Kiltology would be born, a compilation of wisdom, humor, and life experiences that surround donning the kilt. Kevin's kilted passion would lead him to help raise the World's Largest Kilt on the Tulsa Driller. His love for the outdoors and nature helped shape him into an Eagle Scout, community chaperone for the ORRJHS Survival Program since 1988, and Cub Master for his local Cub Scout Pack. His wildly varied life experiences always provide for chuckles, smirks, and, sometimes, some knowledge to those around him. Kevin's deepest passion resides at home where he raises his two children.

www.ingramcontent.com/pod-product-compliance
Lightning Source LLC
Chambersburg PA
CBHW071451070426
42452CB00039B/991